MEADOWS, MANSIONS AND MUNITIONS

Stories and Lives of Cambridge Park

Written and compiled by

Jonathan Crofts

First Published 2021
by Richmond Bridge Media

A CIP record for this book is available from the British Library.
Paperback ISBN 978-1-8382510-0-0
First Edition

Edited (with additional research) by Monica Byles
Cover and page design by Annie Rushton

Printed in England by Pureprint Group on recyclable
materials and using vegetable-based inks.
Front cover postcard image provided by Ashley Hinton.
Back cover images by permission of Richmond upon Thames Borough Art
Collection, Orleans House Gallery and the Howard Webb Collection.

Contents

'From this Terrace one looks down upon the Thames, a sublime translucent Mirrour, on the other side of which are the beautiful meadows of Twickenham, judiciously arranged and adorned by Mr Owen Cambridge their Proprietor, in which is situated his Hospitable Mansion.'

Ozias Humphry, miniaturist and portrait painter, on the view from Richmond Hill
Memoir of Ozias Humphry, c.1802 (Royal Academy of Arts)

What later became known as Cambridge House is on the left. Due to its much-favoured location, with extensive views across the river to Richmond Hill, the house appears in several eighteenth-century paintings and engravings.

Cambridge House can also be seen in 'View of the Thames from Richmond Hill' c.1720-23 by Peter Tillemans (1684–1734) on the Government Art Collection website (www.artcollection.culture.gov.uk).

The Tillemans painting itself once featured in the personal collection of Richard Owen Cambridge, owner of Cambridge House, and was later inherited by his son George Owen Cambridge, Archdeacon of Middlesex.

'The Terrace and View from Richmond Hill' by Leonard Knyff, c. 1720. (By permission of Richmond upon Thames Borough Art Collection, Orleans House Gallery)

Over Richmond Bridge.

FOREWORD by Sir Vince Cable

This wonderful book is a meticulously researched, comprehensive, beautifully illustrated history of that part of Twickenham between Twickenham town and St Margarets to the west, and the river facing Richmond to the east: what is now part of Twickenham Riverside Ward. Jonathan Crofts has managed to unearth just about every photograph, artwork, map and architect's drawing of the area over the last few centuries and has compiled a detailed account of the characters who lived there and shaped its history and geography.

Until the latter part of the nineteenth century, this area was essentially rural with a handful of big houses and their estates. It was known for its meadows. Marble Hill House and Park have been preserved for posterity but others have disappeared, swallowed up in later development. The most important was the Jacobean Cambridge House, whose more famous inhabitants included Richard Owen Cambridge and his son, the Archdeacon Cambridge, who is remembered now for the Twickenham school named after him.

One of its later occupants, Lady Chichester, captured the spirit of the Victorian landowners of Twickenham by successfully holding at bay the arrival of the tram for twenty-five years by petitioning Parliament, claiming that 'it was intolerable to have the ragtag and bobtail disgorged before her Ladyship's house'. Cambridge House, sadly, was demolished in 1937 to make way for redevelopment, as were other landmarks like Haversham Grange and Meadowbank, although the latter was tastefully rebuilt in a modern idiom.

That spirit of aristocratic Nimbyism was in evidence a century earlier when, in 1777, Richmond Bridge was built after fierce resistance from landowners on the Twickenham side and arguments over who should pay (it was tolled to repay the bondholders who financed it). A crucial influence for the building was Horace Walpole, who had protested about the unreliability of the ferry on his journeys into London. The bridge, critically, established a link from fashionable Richmond to sleepy rural Twickenham, which was finally brought into the orbit of London suburbia with the arrival of the train in 1848.

The man who did most to shape today's East Twickenham might now be regarded by some as a 'dodgy developer': Henry Cresswell Foulkes. He built one hundred and sixty Edwardian houses, seven blocks of flats and fifty-four shops, most of which remain, lending the residential area its distinctive character. Unfortunately for him, he went bankrupt in 1908 and has largely been airbrushed out of history, except of course in the name of Cresswell Road. It is also easy to forget the fascinating history of just over a century ago when Twickenham was 'flooded' with immigrants: Belgians, many of them working in a munitions factory close to Richmond Bridge. The area was later home to manufacturing: three-wheeler motorbikes and Reliance Nameplates, which some of us remember for the day nursery that remained when the factory had gone.

The author gives a vivid account of the ice rink, originally envisaged as a roller-skating rink before it emerged as a world-famous centre for ice skating. Most of us are familiar with the Torvill and Dean story, but readers will be fascinated to read that one of the most dedicated skaters for a time was the Nazi war criminal von Ribbentrop, who had a house next door when he was ambassador in London; also the involvement of the royal family, amongst whom Prince Andrew and Princess Anne were devotees. Many of us remember the bitter political quarrels over the rink's closure and it remains an open question as to whether the main responsibility lay with greedy developers, the council, the economics of ice rinks or the vagaries of the planning system.

This otherwise encyclopaedic history does not set out to provide every detail of the political history of the area. When I first stood for Parliament in Twickenham, East Twickenham was an outpost of Richmond and represented by Sir Anthony Royle. Later, the Boundary Commissioners switched it to Twickenham, and I was then privileged to represent it for twenty years.

This book will serve for many years as the definitive history of this part of East Twickenham and today's residents and others will derive pleasure and knowledge from reading about its often surprising heritage.

The Rt. Hon. Sir Vince Cable

The Rt. Hon. Sir Vince Cable represented the area as MP from 1997 to 2015 and 2017 to 2019, and served in the Coalition Cabinet as Secretary of State for Business, Innovation and Skills and President of the Board of Trade from 2010 to 2015.

He has written four books, *Free Radical*, *The Storm*, *After the Storm*, and *Money and Power*, and a novel, *Open Arms*.

A portrait of Sir Vince Cable by Twickenham-based artist Simon Broom

A. The Green
B. The Church
C. Col. Floyder's
D. Col. Duncombe's
E. Dr. Collier's
F. Esq. Mobile's
G. The Road to Clapham
H. The Old Court
I. The River Thames
K. S¹ James Asbur
L. The Frery
M. The Hill
N. The Park
O. Petersham
P. Twickenham
Q. Kingston

THE PROSPECT OF RICHMOND IN SURRY.

INTRODUCTION

'The Prospect of Richmond in Surry', 1726, engraving (unknown) (By permission of Richmond upon Thames Borough Art Collection, Orleans House Gallery) Twickenham Meadows, later Cambridge House, with its formal gardens, and carriage entrance from Ferry Lane, now Richmond Road, is upper right. East Twickenham is otherwise almost undeveloped.

'East Twickenham' may seem a curious label for a collection of streets and houses separated from the rest of Twickenham by the area known as St Margarets. Its origin may derive from the term 'Twickenham East Field', in use during the early seventeenth century. Its residents today certainly think of the area as quite separate, with its own distinct flavour and characteristics.

This book focusses on the area to the south of Richmond Road, which provides its northern boundary. To the east and south it is bounded by Richmond Bridge and the Thames, and to the west by Marble Hill Park. More about the history of Marble Hill House and Park, an English Heritage property under renovation in 2020–21, can be found on the English Heritage website (www.english-heritage. org.uk) and in other publications.

The history of the upper part of East Twickenham, to the north of Richmond Road, has been documented in large part by the Twickenham Park Residents Association, publicly available on its website (www.twickenhampark.co.uk).

Twickenham Park itself was the first great estate on this side of the river, harking back to royal connections in Elizabethan times: Francis Bacon (1561–1626), Lord Verulam, a favourite of Elizabeth I, lived here and created a garden of some renown. There would undoubtedly have been contact between this and the Twickenham Meadows estate, of slightly later date, just to the south, which eventually became Cambridge Park. Just over the river lay the Palace of Shene (subsequently renamed as Richmond Palace, where Queen Elizabeth died in 1603), and four miles upstream was the Palace at Hampton Court.

The wider district, including on the Richmond side of the river, was home to many famous artists, such as Joshua Reynolds and J M W Turner, who painted views of the country mansions of their day, charting the various stages of development of East Twickenham over the last four hundred years. Turner's own country residence, Sandycombe Lodge in St Margarets, is sited just beyond the scope of this book; more information can be found on the Turner's House Trust website (www.turnershouse.org). A fine selection of Turner's views from Richmond Hill is available on the Tate website (www.tate.org.uk).

Indeed, once it became more broadly established, this fortunate part of London has played host to a wide gathering of fascinating individuals. In the last hundred years alone, residents of the Cambridge Park estate in its many guises have included a distinguished WWI Field Marshal and other senior officers from the armed forces; a theatre impresario and star of the Victorian and Edwardian music hall as well as the silver screen; significant business leaders; modern TV and film celebrities. Many others of lower public profile have contributed enormously to the daily lives and satisfactions of the local community.

Today, East Twickenham is an affluent suburb adjoining the Thames, technically on the north bank of the river because of how it curves, but a distinct part of south-west London and Richmond Borough. The proximity of this major waterway and the many green spaces in the borough, plus easy access to public transport (bus services, along with the Tube and railway network from Richmond Station) make it a desirable place to live. This is reflected in property prices, so that like much of the borough, its population includes a high proportion of middle-class professionals, as well as a contingent of media and entertainment industry workers of various sorts, both on-screen and off-screen talent. Many families live here, alongside single people and retired couples, and there is a marked international mix.

This twenty-first century blend of individuals of all nationalities in some ways runs counter to the 'strong sense of Englishness' that was so evident during Twickenham's campaign to secure borough status a century earlier: the procession from Richmond Bridge to York House on Charter Day in 1926 was accompanied by supporters with flags and bunting, and an apparent desire to link Twickenham with the British royal family, rather than the French and Portuguese dynasties who already had connections here. The community also demonstrated a very tangible patriotism and love of Empire through to the Second World War, common to most folk of this era.

Richmond Road follows the path of an ancient track from Church Street in central Twickenham to the ferry over to Richmond. It ran across what was then the Great East Field and along the southern boundary of Twickenham Park, the neighbouring great estate on this side of the river. By the eighteenth century this approach to the ferry was known as Ferry Lane. When Richmond Bridge was completed in 1777, it became known as Richmond Road. The trams that ran here from Twickenham and elsewhere at the start of the twentieth century were never able to use the bridge due to engineering constraints, such as its steep gradient. Richmond Bridge remained an obstacle to improving circulation of traffic locally, and this finally led to the construction of Twickenham Bridge to support the new A316 trunk road in 1933.

From one perspective, the neighbourhood has long lived a little in the shadow of central Richmond, just over the bridge, with its theatres, cinemas, restaurants, bars and galleries. But East Twickenham had its own screen entertainments in the early part of the twentieth century, specifically the Gaiety Picture Playhouse, later known as the Gaiety Cinema. This closed in 1930 and the building became the Temperance Billiard Hall until the 1950s.

Despite modern-day appearances, manufacturing and engineering have featured heavily in local history: during the World War I period, a munitions factory was established by the Belgian engineer Charles Pelabon. This site had had a chequered history, originally planned as a roller-skating rink, then as a bus garage, before becoming a centre for employment of a whole community of Belgian refugees: the 'Belgian Village on the Thames'. In the late 1920s, part of the site became what was popularly known as Richmond Ice Rink, until contentious redevelopment into luxury residences in the late 1990s. Munitions also featured in the early history of the Beaufort Works, next to Marble Hill Park. Engineering and other businesses were to continue on both sites, until later replacement by residential accommodation.

In the seventeenth and eighteenth centuries, the land had been one of the largest riverside estates in the Twickenham area. The mansion built in the 1600s near the

Richmond Road, East Twickenham, Charter Day, 22 September 1926, when Twickenham's status was elevated from Urban District to Municipal Borough. The Charter was handed to the Mayor by the Home Secretary at Richmond Bridge, and processed through to York House. (Howard Webb Collection)

old Richmond ferry (where Richmond Bridge was later constructed) was originally known as Twickenham Meadows. This was later acquired by the Cambridge family, headed by Richard Owen Cambridge, and after his death was renamed Cambridge House – his name persists throughout this corner of London and the Thames, and he is perhaps its most notable personage, due to his wide-ranging talents and society connections.

It is to be regretted perhaps that a fine Jacobean mansion of such quality, having survived for over three hundred years, is not still there for us to see. Surrounded by recent suburban development, lack of funds for its maintenance led to its final demise in 1937. Although Richard Owen Cambridge continues as a subject for literary and academic study, it is likely that his reputation as one of the 'Twickenham Luminaries' would be more widely established had his former home survived to the current day, similar to that, for example, of Horace Walpole at Strawberry Hill.

The Thames Landscape Strategy, of whom local resident Sir David Attenborough is patron, confirms that 'The traditional habitat along the Thames has, for centuries, been water meadows that are either cut for hay or grazed by cattle. Although these meadows are entirely man-made, they provide a rich and varied home for a diversity of plant life and are now one of the most endangered habitats in the UK… Two of the best places to view these special places are at Syon Park and Petersham Meadow.'

The Cambridge estate was finally divided in 1835, but the theme of meadows was to linger in the names of two properties to the south: Meadow Bank and Meadowside Cottage. Meadow Bank was sold to an astronomer who built an observatory in its grounds. The site was later used for The Exiles Club, providing a London base and recuperation for employees of Cable and Wireless Ltd, originally

An engraving by John Landseer, based on a drawing by John Webber, of Twickenham Meadows, later known as Cambridge House, 1803. Richmond Bridge is to the right. Constructed of red brick on three floors, the house had a flat front to the east side, facing the river, with formal gardens enclosed by a fence or wall from the towpath and Ferry Lane. (By permission of Richmond upon Thames Borough Art Collection, Orleans House Gallery)

a group of telegraph companies providing communications across the Empire, and of great significance during the two world wars. Meadow Bank, still with its original name, returned to residential use in 1999, sharing its site with the new Lynde House Care Home. Incidentally, Lynde too is a reference to the original owner of what later became Cambridge House.

From the seventeenth century onwards, the wealthy who wanted to escape London built their rural retreats along the Middlesex bank of the river; they revelled in glorious summer entertainments by the riverside, and the tradition of the Arcadian Thames persists to this day. With the advent of the railway in the late nineteenth and early twentieth centuries, Twickenham's expansion as a suburb blossomed and it became popular with Londoners to visit and enjoy this stretch of the Thames, with walks leading from Richmond Bridge to Marble Hill House and Park and beyond, just like today.

During the reign of Queen Victoria, it is estimated that close to six million houses were built throughout England. Rapid population growth, accompanied by migration to the cities, produced a huge demand for housing which was met through the work of thousands of small speculative construction companies. This was much the case in East Twickenham, where builders from the Little and Foulkes families transformed the former Cambridge Park estate into what we see now.

Property changes in the twenty-first century will continue to drive more change in the feel and composition of the area. In 2021, a new supermarket and a primary school open in Richmond Road, in the redevelopment of the site of a former office building. The school will help service the growing younger population of this part of London, and the supermarket will bring benefits but also a mixed impact on the traders along local roads. The full effects are yet to materialise.

In political terms, East Twickenham is now part of Twickenham Riverside ward, which stretches further to the north and west, and is represented by three councillors in the London Borough of Richmond upon Thames. The council has a long Liberal (Democrat) and Conservative tradition, its leadership switching between the two parties since its inception in 1965, as the parliamentary constituency has also done since 2015.

It remains to be seen what further changes will result following the Covid-19 crisis, and indeed any ongoing effects from Brexit from the European Union. As the UK and the wider world slowly recover from the 2020–21 pandemic in economic and social terms, community spirit seems likely to play an even stronger role in the area, which by London standards is already friendly and welcoming. Public gatherings and events should slowly return. Working practices may well change for ever, with those who can continuing to work from home. Environmental concerns may help encourage the preservation and enhancement of the remnants and successors of the ancient meadows that once lay at the heart of what is now East Twickenham.

This book records four centuries of stories and lives in an area that has played a significant role in the social and artistic development of the London metropolis. The coming decades will likely produce many more tales of fascinating people, buildings and events, adding to our rich cultural heritage.

Only time will tell.

A West View of Richmond &c in Surry from the Star and Garter on the Hill ¶ Vûe du lé sté de l'Occident de Richmond &c. dans Surry prise de l'Enseigne de l'Etoile et de la Jarretiere.

London Printed for & Sold by Rich.d Sayer at the Golden Buck opposite Fetter Lane Fleet Street.

CHAPTER 1
ARTISTS AND PERSPECTIVES

East Twickenham and St Margarets form a core part of the view from Richmond Hill in Surrey – the only English landscape view that is protected by an Act of Parliament. Since the late seventeenth century, artists have been attracted by the panoramic prospect of the meandering River Thames set amongst verdant woods and meadows offered from this elevated position. Their paintings have recorded the changes to the landscape, the growth of trees, and the introduction of new villas such as Marble Hill House to the existing mansions, including Twickenham Meadows, later to be Cambridge House on the Cambridge Park estate.

When suburban development threatened Marble Hill in the early twentieth century, it was prevented by a determined campaign that centred on preserving this celebrated viewpoint. Meanwhile, much of the Cambridge Park estate was being built over at around the same period. English Heritage have studied a number of historical paintings of this area, and their analysis is woven into this chapter.

By the mid-eighteenth century, fashionable Richmond was attracting a wide range of artists and engravers, who produced a plethora of views, not only of Richmond

A West View of Richmond &c in Surry from the Star and Garter on the Hill, a print published c.1752 after the drawing by Augustin Heckel. Twickenham Meadows, later Cambridge House, is centre left, facing the river. (By permission of Richmond upon Thames Borough Art Collection, Orleans House Gallery)

but also of Twickenham and the surrounding area. Prominent among local artists was Augustin Heckel, a German-born goldsmith who, having retired to Richmond as a wealthy man in 1746, turned his hand to topographical views of the area. Heckel's detailed drawings, engraved during his lifetime and afterwards, provide some of the most valuable records of Richmond and Twickenham, including scenes of the river, the Hill, and the nearby royal deer park.

Heckel was born in Augsburg, the son of a chaser (someone who form designs by pressing into metal), and worked in gold and silver; he worked in many major German cities before travelling to Paris and then moving to England. He also created topographical views in watercolour, some of which were copied by the engraver Thomas Bowles and published by Robert Sayer, as well as eight small plates of Richmond and its environs. Heckel died in Richmond in 1770.

A View from Richmond Hill looking South-West, by Antonio Joli, c.1750 (By permission of Richmond upon Thames Borough Art Collection, Orleans House Gallery)

The precise and detailed topographical style introduced into Britain by Dutch and Flemish artists is clearly demonstrated in the work of the Italian-born and -trained painter Antonio Joli (1700–77). Marble Hill House, built in the 1720s, is visible in his work, *A View from Richmond Hill looking South-West*. Recognisable from the triangular pediment on its roofline, the house lies over the river from the famous viewpoint, to the right of the canvas. To its left sits a large building with a distinctive octagonal pavilion – that part at least still known to us today. At the time this was the home of the MP George Pitt, known since 1815 as Orleans House after its famous resident Louis Philippe, Duc d'Orléans (1773–1850).

The village of Twickenham lies a little further off along the riverbank. The mansion in front and to the left of Marble Hill House is believed to represent Cambridge House, although with some minor artistic licence with the geography. This view was painted in about 1750, when Marble Hill was still home to Henrietta Howard, mistress of George II, and Twickenham Meadows was yet to be rechristened as Cambridge House. Henrietta Howard was acquainted with her new neighbour, Richard Owen Cambridge, who bought the property some months later in 1751.

A drawing by Jean Baptiste Claude Chatelain (1710–58) shows a similar view from about 1755. Drawn from the lower vantage point of the Summer House in Richmond Park, Marble Hill now lies at the centre of the scene. Little is shown of Twickenham Meadows house and estate, off to the right. The elegant couple exclaiming at the vista in the foreground and the pleasure barge on the river are reminders of the popularity of this prospect among eighteenth-century visitors. The view was sketched with the permission of Princess Amelia, second daughter of George II, who became Ranger of Richmond Park in 1751 and restricted public access to the park until 1758.

A View from the Summer House in Richmond Park up the River Thames, c.1819
Drawing by Jean Baptiste Claude Chatelain (1710–58), engraved by Peter Paul Benazech (c.1730–1798)
(By permission of Richmond upon Thames Borough Art Collection, Orleans House Gallery)

A View from the Summer House in Richmond Park Up the River Thames. Taken by permission of Her Royal Highness the princess Amelia. / Vüe prise du Pavillon dans le Parc de Richmond en remontant la Tamise. Dessiné avec la permission de feu Altesse Royale Madame la princesse Amelie.

Printed for R Wilkinson, at N°58 in Cornhill, London.

By contrast, the houses on the far riverbank are barely visible at all in the view of *The Thames from Richmond Hill*, painted in 1788 by Sir Joshua Reynolds (1723–1792), who was more interested in composition and tone than precise detail. Reynolds, who became the first president of the newly established Royal Academy in 1768, is better known as a portrait painter, but this landscape held a special appeal for him. He owned Wick House on Richmond Hill from 1771, which he used as a place to entertain guests, away from the filth and hubbub of late eighteenth-century life in the city of London. His home was designed by Sir William Chambers and rejoiced in a fine bow window on the first floor, from which Reynolds could admire the full panorama over the Thames.

For his painting, Reynolds chose a viewpoint between Wick House and The Star and Garter tavern which had opened in 1738. The inn was a fairly modest affair, built on the site of the current-day Star and Garter apartments. Another of Reynolds' close neighbours on the crest of Richmond Hill was his artistic rival, Thomas Gainsborough (1727–1788), who leased No. 2 The Terrace towards the end of his life.

Reynolds was a frequent visitor at Twickenham Meadows, Richard Owen Cambridge's home on the Twickenham side of the river, subsequently renamed after its owner. It seems that his host greatly admired the great artist, publicly writing of his '… superior taste and execution … no less than his amiable manners, and extensive knowledge of all subjects, that can engage an elegant mind.'

A reverse view, from Twickenham riverside, shows the extent of the buildings on Richmond Hill itself in a *View of the Terrace, Richmond Hill*, painted in about 1780 by William Marlow (1740/41–1813). From the end of the seventeenth century onwards, this was a prestigious place to live, with notable houses including No. 3 The Terrace, built in 1767 for the playing card manufacturer Christopher Blanchard, and subsequently lived in by Mrs Fitzherbert, illicit wife of George IV. There were also places for entertainment and refreshments, with a theatre open from 1719 and several taverns, such as the Roebuck with its fine view from the Terrace promenade, beloved haunt of many since its opening in around 1715.

View of the Terrace, Richmond Hill, by William Marlow, c.1780 (By permission of Richmond upon Thames Borough Art Collection, Orleans House Gallery)

Marlow was a successful landscape painter who produced many views of this stretch of the Thames. He had moved to the Manor House in Twickenham in about 1775 where his mentor, the marine painter Samuel Scott (1702–1772), had previously lived. The last vestige of this once fine Tudor building finally came down in 1934 on the corner of Church Street and Arragon Road, where the modern-day Arragon House and its neighbours now stand.

Twickenham and Richmond were a veritable hive of artistic activity in the late eighteenth and early nineteenth centuries. In 1814, this area became the home of one of Britain's greatest landscape painters, J M W Turner (1775–1851), who designed and built for himself and his father Sandycombe Lodge (now No. 40 Sandycoombe Road, Twickenham, run by the Turner's House Trust), very close to Marble Hill and the Cambridge Park area. Turner painted much of the local Thames geography, and made frequent excursions to Richmond Hill.

His large-scale oil painting, *Thomson's Aeolian Harp*, first exhibited in 1809, is perhaps the most celebrated painting looking from the top of the Hill and over the vale. In the foreground he introduced an imaginary classical monument – the harp of Aeolus, god of the winds in Greek mythology. On the pedestal of the monument, Turner painted the name 'THOMSON'. This is a reference to the eighteenth-century Richmond poet James Thomson (1700–48), who described the view in his poem 'Summer' from *The Seasons*, first published in 1727 – the building works at Marble Hill were underway, and Sir James Ashe was owner of Twickenham Meadows, later known as Cambridge House. The poem invites us to:

> 'trace the matchless vale of Thames;
> Far-winding up to where the muses haunt
> To Twit'nam's bowers'.

Today, the painting can be seen at the Manchester Art Gallery or on its website (www.manchesterartgallery.org).

Turner also painted the watercolours *Richmond Hill* (c.1820–25) and *Richmond Terrace* (1836), from higher up the Hill, which both show more of the Cambridge Park estate land on the right of the paintings, populated by tiny figures. These are in the collections of the Lady Lever and Walker Art Galleries (National Museums Liverpool) and as engravings elsewhere, including in the Royal Academy and British Museum in London. (See also Chapter 16.)

A View from Richmond Hill, by Thomas Christopher Hofland, c.1820 (By permission of Richmond upon Thames Borough Art Collection, Orleans House Gallery)

By the nineteenth century, Marble Hill was no longer visible from Richmond Hill, having been screened by trees. *A View from Richmond Hill*, painted by Thomas Christopher Hofland in about 1820 when he lived next to Marble Hill in Montpelier Row, shows only Little Marble Hill, the small white house among the trees on the distant bank of the river.

Known in the eighteenth century as Marble Hill Cottage, this house lay at the south-eastern corner of the Marble Hill estate, closer to the Thames than the main house, and on the edge of the Cambridge Park estate. It was let to a succession of tenants, including Lady Diana Beauclerk, daughter of the 3rd Duke of Marlborough, who lived there between 1782 and 1789, and was the preferred residence of Henrietta Howard's great-niece, Henrietta Hotham, when she inherited the estate in 1793. Little Marble Hill was demolished about 1873/4.

Again, little of the Cambridge Park estate is shown to the left on the East Twickenham bank, despite the fact that Cambridge House itself survived until 1937. The building stood on the eastern side of the present-day Cambridge Road, off Richmond Road near Richmond Bridge. It was later encroached upon all sides by the growth of suburban East Twickenham, although Cambridge Gardens, the Warren Footpath along the river, and leafy Cambridge Park road all hark back to the bucolic setting of the original 'Arcadian Thames'.

The story of the Cambridge Park estate preserves the essence of a pastoral paradise very much still present in this semi-suburbia created some hundred and twenty years ago.

A slightly later 'View from Richmond Hill', 1830, by Edmund John Niemann (1813–1876) showing a still heavily wooded Middlesex bank (By permission of Richmond upon Thames Borough Art Collection, Orleans House Gallery)

CHAPTER 2

ARISTOCRATS AND ENCLOSURES

The land occupied by the Cambridge Park estate originally belonged to the Manor of Isleworth, granted in 1227 by Henry III to his younger brother Richard, Earl of Cornwall. In 1594, Elizabeth I appointed Henry Percy, 9th Earl of Northumberland, to the position of Steward of the Manor of Isleworth, at the same time granting him the lease of what is now Syon House and Park. Ten years later, in 1604, in recognition of the Earl's services in furthering his succession to the throne, James I granted the house and manor to the Earl of Northumberland and his heirs in perpetuity. Cambridge Park remained in copyhold to the Manor of Isleworth Syon until the enfranchisement of part of it in 1860, and of the remainder in 1886.

Copyhold was one of the three main forms of land ownership found in the postmedieval period. Freehold corresponds to ownership in the modern sense, and leasehold refers to property held on a lease for a fixed period from a freeholder. Copyhold property belonged to the lord of the manor, and was held from him by the de facto owner. It had developed from medieval 'customary' tenure (holding, according to the custom of the manor) because changes of ownership were made in the manor court and recorded on the court rolls. The new owner received a copy of the roll entry to prove his tenancy.

The 1635 map by Moses Glover – Richmond and the Cambridge Park area are centre left (Syon House, Collection of the Duke of Northumberland)

The first evidence of an enclosure in the Twickenham East Field is shown on a map drawn by Ralph Treswell the Younger in 1607, 'A Plott of the Whole Manor of Sion within the Countie of Middlesex belonging to the rt honorable the Earl of Northumberland'. This map shows two enclosures adjoining Twickenham Park. The first, close to the ferry, marked 'Richard Brome'. Upstream and immediately adjoining is a larger enclosure, marked 'Mr. Poole', and a small building is shown in the north-east corner.

By 1635, further development can be seen on a map held at Syon House, Brentford. Part map, part drawing, of the 'Istelworth Hunderd calculated and described by Moses Glover paynter and Architectur', the detail includes land measurements and drawings of principal buildings. The two enclosures shown in Treswell's map appear to have merged, and there is now a house of some considerable size, together with adjacent outbuildings, set in 3 acres and ascribed to 'Ye Countesse of Totnesse'. A 15-acre field adjoining, described as sandy, is marked 'Ye Warrine planted and ye house builded by Mr. Grimse Rich finished by Sir Humphrey Line Kt'.

There is evidence of the existence of a warren in the Twickenham East Field in a survey of Twickenham Park taken in 1562, with reference to 'A peace of grounde called the Old Warren'. A warren was the name given to land over which a right to hunt had been granted, but by the seventeenth century the name had come to be more specifically used in connection with the breeding of rabbits and hares (both referred to as 'coney'). As there is no mention of any warren-type activity in later maps, it would appear that, with the building of the house, the use of the warren for breeding rabbits was discontinued and the land put to more 'gentlemanly' uses.

Twickenham Meadows, later known as Cambridge Park, was a 74-acre estate, the second largest estate in Twickenham after Twickenham Park. The estate lands surrounded a three-storey Jacobean mansion, built from brick around 1610 and later known as Cambridge House (pictured here in 1905). It was demolished in 1937. (Howard Webb Collection)

Cambridge House, Richmond Bridge.

The name, however, continued to be applied. '50 acres of copyhold land in Warren Close or the Old Warren' were listed as part of a Conditional Surrender by Joseph Windham Ashe on the 21st April 1742, and in 1818 the Commissioners for the Twickenham Enclosure awarded the Revd George Owen Cambridge 'the piece of land adjoining the mansion house … measuring 40a 0r 14p named "The Warren"'. The river path from Richmond Bridge to the southern end of Orleans Road is still known as the Warren Footpath today.

The exact date of construction of the house is not known but it is assumed that building was complete and Sir Humphrey Lynd (or Lynde, or Line) was in residence by the time of the baptism of his daughter Anna, recorded in the parish register on 25 March 1617. Moses Glover's map shows a rectangular house adorned with turrets, facing the river, and this is confirmed by later paintings and engravings. From the north-west corner of the boundary, where it adjoined Twickenham Park, a track or footpath led across the fields to Twickenham village. This path would also have been used by travellers to Twickenham who had crossed from Richmond by means of the ferry.

Sir Humphrey Lynd, owner, c.1616–1630

Sir Humphrey Lynd was a 'most learned knight and zealous puritan', who devoted his life to the cause of religion, writing energetically against the Church of Rome and arousing strong opposition.

Born of a Dorset family in 1579, he was knighted by James I in 1613, and came to Twickenham around 1616. The baptisms of five children of Sir Humphrey and 'Margaret his ladie' are recorded in the parish registers: Anna on 25 March 1617, followed by Margaret on 15 November 1618, Jane on 31 May 1620, Katherine on 24 September 1621 and Humphrey on 26 July 1626.

Sir Humphrey succeeded to a family estate near Cobham in Surrey, where he moved with his family in around 1630. After a painful illness, 'testifying with his last breath his constancy to the reformed church', he died on the 8th June 1636 and lies buried in the parish church of Cobham.

The Twickenham house, an imposing Jacobean mansion, was built in parklands that extended to 74 acres. The boundaries are well defined, formed to the north and west by the Richmond Road from the foot of the bridge to the Rising Sun public house, and to the south and west by Marble Hill. To the east, the frontage along the River Thames swept from the Richmond Bridge of today to the boundary with Marble Hill.

Built only a few years later than Ham House across the river, Cambridge House contained at least twenty-six rooms, according to the Hearth Tax returns. The Hearth Assessment for Lady Day 1664 showed that tax was paid on twenty-six hearths, although in 1672 this was adjusted to twenty-five. Neighbouring Twickenham Park to the north, by comparison, was taxed in the same years on the basis of thirty-five hearths and at the time was the third largest house in the Isleworth Hundred.

According to an inventory taken prior to demolition in 1937, the interior of the house contained 'some fine rooms as well as two magnificently carved pillars of great value and matchless beauty'. (See Chapter 15 for a photo of the impressive entrance hall described on the next page.)

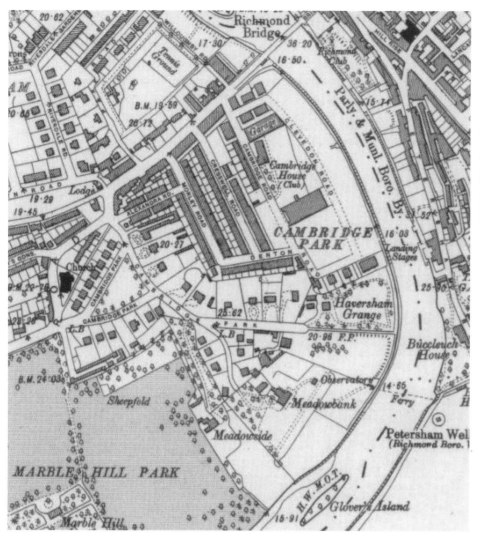

Ordnance Survey map of 1935 (revised 1933), shortly before the demolition of Cambridge House, showing the boundaries of the Cambridge Park estate: Richmond Road, running south-west from Richmond Bridge, Marble Hill Park, and the Thames (Reproduced with the permission of the National Library of Scotland)

It further stated that: 'the entrance hall has a fireplace with an early to mid-17th century surround, reset; it is flanked by terminal female pilasters, supporting a frieze and a gadrooned shelf; the frieze has four carved panels of the labours of Hercules, masks and draped female figures; four doors in the same room have reset late 17th century overdoors carved with foliage, flowers, children, and an eagle.

'A window on the staircase has 16th century foreign painted glass with three shields-of-arms set in an architectural framing. At the south end of the house is a reset early 18th century staircase with turned balusters and close strings. Condition: Good'.

A local historian, inspecting the property during demolition, wrote: 'The panelling of this room (a bedroom, one of the largest rooms in the house) consisted of 17th century pine ... behind the panelling was a sequence of coloured frescoes ... one which I saw was nearly a square yard in extent. In general outline the frescoes seem to have been arched. They include a fleur-de-lys … with lovebirds or winged doves in the spanrail. The design of the frescoes is early pendant, with conventional terminals, and the various colourings are pale brown, dark brown, light green and pale yellow.

'In the main drawing room … the mantelpiece … was of pine heavily carved and upon removal disclosed an earlier fire surround in carved Portland stone. This carved stonework was of beautiful workmanship and design and consisted in the main of Tudor roses and festoons of flowers and fruit. It was in a splendid state of preservation, being protected in the last years by the mantel. The inside members also of Portland stone were reeded and fluted. The mantelpiece surrounded an old dog grate. Upon expert examination this dog-grate proved to be enriched with hallmarked chased silver, and its value is estimated to be in excess of £500.'

The Countess of Totness, owner, c.1630–1637

The Countess of Totness came to Twickenham following the death of her husband in 1629. Her choice of house may have been influenced by her prior knowledge of the area, as her husband had acted as trustee for Lucy, Countess of Bedford, in the purchase of Twickenham Park in 1608.

The Countess was the elder daughter and co-heiress of William Clopton, who owned the Manor of Clopton in Warwickshire. Joyce Clopton was baptised at Stratford-upon-Avon on 17 September 1562, and at the age of fifteen married George Carew, second son of the Dean of Windsor and kinsman of Sir Walter Raleigh. George Carew was twenty-five years old, an adventurous Elizabethan and a 'sworn servant' to the Queen. Within three months of the marriage he was sent to Ireland as a Captain of Foot, where he witnessed the death 'most butcherlie' of his elder brother, and 'had the good hap to kill him that slew my brother' a few weeks later.

In 1582, Carew had again to leave his young wife, this time for Flanders with the Duke of Anjou, returning to Ireland the following year, when he further avenged his brother's killing by 'murdering on Midsummers Eve 1583, Owen O'Nasye in Dublin'. This act of violence does not appear to have affected either his standing or his future, for he was knighted in Ireland in 1586, and was later appointed Commander of Inquiry of Spanish Wrecks in Ireland at the time of the Armada.

After many years in Ireland, and long separations when Sir George sailed on voyages of exploration as Master of Ordnance to the Earl of Essex and as Vice Admiral to Sir Walter Raleigh, the Carews returned to England in 1603.

Sir George was elevated to the peerage in 1605 and assumed the title of Baron Carew of Clopton, his wife having inherited the Manor of Clopton from her father; in 1625, he was created Earl of Totness. As Treasurer and Receiver-General, he served the wife of Charles I, Queen Henrietta Maria, from 1616 until his death in London in 1629.

After his death, the Countess came to spend her declining years in Twickenham, where she died on 14 January 1637. Her body was then taken to Stratford-upon-Avon for burial alongside her husband in a tomb 'splendid in alabaster and coloured marbles … their recumbent effigies (coloured) he dressed in armour and she in a red dress with a fur-lined red mantle, both wearing coronets.'

There were no children of the marriage, although the Earl was reputed to have fathered 'an almost certain illegitimate son, Sir Thomas Stafford', and by her will, the Countess left her house and lands in Twickenham to 'my dearly beloved niece Ursula Clopton daughter of my sister Ann Clopton'. Her personal estate was valued at £20,000. With no desire to leave Warwickshire and move to Twickenham, Ursula Clopton sold the house 'close bye the Richmond ferry', along with seventeen parcels of land, including land in Long Sandborough Close and in the Old Warren, to Sir Thomas Lawley Bt., in 1638.

Sir Thomas Lawley, Bt., owner, 1638–1646

Sir Thomas Lawley came from an old established family of Spoonhill in Shropshire. He had been apprenticed to Edward Rotherham, a London draper, and spent some years in the Low Countries from 1607, eventually as a merchant adventurer specialising in 'Spanish cloth' (made in England with Spanish wool). He returned to London in May 1623, and inherited his eldest brother's estate at Spoonhill in 1624, becoming very wealthy through this inheritance and his business dealings.

He sat as Member of Parliament for Wenlock between 1625 and 1629, although little is recorded of his parliamentary activities, and was created a Baronet on 16 August 1641, the same year that he was appointed as an Alderman of the City of London. He chose to remain in London where his business was based during the Civil War period, avoiding Shropshire which had declared its support for the Royalists. While Master of the Draper's Company in 1642–1643, he was obliged to pay £800 towards Parliament's costs during the war (with a later reduction of £200), after which he returned to Holland for a short interlude.

Sir Thomas died at Twickenham on 19 October 1646, leaving a widow, Anne (who subsequently married Sir John Glynne, Lord Chief Justice of the Upper Bench) and three children: Francis (who succeeded to the title and also inherited the Shropshire estates), Elizabeth and Thomas. Their father was buried in Twickenham Church, where a handsome tablet recorded his death in Latin. He left £7,000 in goods to his younger children and Anne.

Some eleven years lapsed between the death of Sir Thomas Lawley and the admittance in the Court Rolls for 1657 of his youngest son Thomas to sixteen parcels of land, commencing with 'the messuage pigeon house barns stables gardens etc near Richmond Ferry', and including the Old Warren, East Field, Marble Hole and Dole Mead. Having acquired the property, young Thomas lost no time in immediately disposing of it, and the same entry in the Court Rolls records the transfer of the house and other lands to Joseph Ash [sic], later Sir Joseph Ashe, who took possession of the mansion which was then to be the home of the Ashe family of merchants for nearly one hundred years.

CHAPTER 3
MERCHANTS AND MORTGAGES

Sir Joseph Ashe, owner, 1657–1686

Sir Joseph Ashe was a wealthy merchant who supported the Royalist cause during the Civil War. On the restoration to the throne of Charles II, his services (which were mainly financial) were acknowledged and he was created a baronet in September 1660.

Born in Somerset in 1617, the third surviving son of James Ashe Esquire, a clothier, Sir Joseph was descended from the 'ancient and eminent family of Esse, Ashe or D'Essecourt, which came over with William the Conqueror'.

Oil painting on canvas of Sir Joseph Ashe, 1st Bt. (1617–1686) by Sir Peter Lely (1618–1680) and studio, c.1660–1665. (© National Trust Images)

Around 1650, he married Mary, the daughter of Robert Wilson, a London draper. She was fourteen years his junior, and bore him nine children, two sons and seven daughters, of whom five survived to adulthood. Their first child, Joseph, died in infancy. Katherine, Mary and Anne were born before their parents moved to Twickenham, and Martha was the first of their children to be baptised in the parish church, in 1658. Grace was buried in 1665 (the same year in which twenty-four people in Twickenham died of the plague), Diana was baptised in 1666 and died in 1676, and Elizabeth died in 1669 at the age of five. The last child and only son, James, was born in 1674, by which time both parents were well into their middle age – Sir Joseph was by then fifty-six, and Lady Ashe forty-two.

Sir Joseph was well established in business before he brought his wife and family to Twickenham. His connections were mainly with the Low Countries, particularly Antwerp, where he came to the rescue of the Duchess of Newcastle. The impoverished Duke and his wife had been in exile for many years, living mainly on credit, and upon the Restoration, the Duke immediately returned to attend the Court in England, leaving the poor Duchess stranded in their house in Antwerp as 'a pawn for his debts'. Many months passed and it was only through the generosity of a substantial loan from Sir Joseph of more than £3,000 that these debts were finally discharged, enabling the Duchess to make a dignified departure.

Sir Joseph now turned his attention to the acquisition of land and during the family's early years in Twickenham, he extended the grounds attached to the mansion and bought holdings throughout the parish. A Survey of the Parish taken on 25 March 1661 showed him as the owner of 'A dwellinghouse and 49 acres of land belonging to ye house; 118 acres of lands bought of Mr. Pitcarne and 16 acres of lands bought of William Ossifer'. (Charles Pitcarne was a fellow churchwarden of St Mary's along with Sir Joseph Ashe.)

A Commission of Inquiry into the landholdings in Twickenham appointed by Charles II in 1668–1669 revealed that 'within the last twenty years, he (Sir Joseph) has enclosed several parts of Eastfield' (22 acres according to one witness) and also that 'the King's Highway leading to Richmond Ferry from Twickenham has been turned and altered within this twelve month by Sir Joseph Ashe'. This accounts for the 'dogleg' in the present-day Richmond Road by the Rising Sun opposite Marble Hill Park, curving round past St Stephen's Church to the traffic lights, where it turns sharp right and straightens out towards Richmond Bridge. Further evidence given to the Commission stated that 'Sir Joseph Ash's house lies on the further part of Eastfield' and that 'Eastfield extends near to Twickenham Parish and most of the houses thereabouts lie in Eastfield and many houses have been built in his time'.

The Hearth Tax return for 1674 shows Sir Joseph Ashe as the owner of four houses, other than the mansion house, empty at the time of assessment, the largest taxed on ten hearths, and the others on three, five and three. It is not clear which buildings these represent.

By 1681, Sir Joseph Ashe appears to have assumed responsibility for the meadow known as Ferry Mead, adjacent to Richmond Ferry and Ferry Lane, and previously enclosed by the owner of Twickenham Park. Between 1611 and 1617, the sum of 40s a year was paid to the parish by the Countess of Bedford, then resident at Twickenham Park, but after she moved away this payment lapsed. A memorandum in the vestry records of 1640 stated that 'the 40s per annum has not been paid for the last twelve years' and on 18 September 1648 an order was made 'that if the owners of Twickenham Park and the Ferry Mead do not make good all arrears due according to a former agreement in the taking of the said Ferry Mead, it should be lawful for the parishioners to put in their cattle the Michaelmas following'.

The overseer's account for 1673 shows receipt of a sum of 20s, and the vestry book for 1681 stated that 'in consideration of the keeping and inclosing of Ferry Mead free from pasture in common, there was paid to this parish 40 shillings a year; but now no more is received than 20s a year, which is received of Sir Joseph Ashe, Baronet.' This annual sum continued to be paid by the owners of Cambridge House until the end of the nineteenth century.

During the seventeenth and eighteenth centuries, the land subsequently formed one of the largest riverside estates in Twickenham, second only in size to its neighbour, Twickenham Park.

From the early eighteenth century, the main gates to the estate stood in Ferry Lane, which was to become an important highway with the opening of Richmond Bridge in 1777 and is today the Richmond Road.

Sir Joseph disposed of several plots of land to the parish, for the ultimate benefit of the poor. In 1681, 'in consideration of £120 (he) conveyed to Nathaniel Axtell and others of the parish of Twickenham and their heirs, a parcel of meadow ground in Twickenham containing by estimation 6 acres in a meadow called More Mead ... upon trust to permit the Vestry to let and dispose of the same ... the rent and profits of the said piece of land were to be disposed of for the use of the poor ... as the Vestry should think fit'.

An entry in the parish ledger for 8 May 1681 contains a copy of the receipt by Sir Joseph Ashe of £100 in full for acres of land in Mother Ivy's Shott. This sum consisted of £50 in cash and the remainder as a gift to the parish of 12d a week, to supply the defect of 'a gift of £5. 4s. 0d to be bestowed in wheaten bread every Sabbath' by one Lewis Owen of Twickenham, who had failed to leave sufficient funds to discharge it.

John Rocque's Survey of London 1741–1745 showing the Cambridge Park estate. Richmond Ferry and Ferry Lane (later Richmond Road) can be seen at the top. The Twickenham Meadows house and associated buildings sit just beneath. (Image from Twickenham Museum)

While Sir Joseph was enlarging his estate in Twickenham, he was also acquiring property and land in Yorkshire and in Wiltshire. In 1661, he leased the Manor of Downton from the Bishop of Winchester and in 1670 was elected Member of Parliament for the borough, a position he held until his death, after which it passed to his heir Sir James Ashe, who sat between 1701 and 1705.

Local affairs also played a part in Sir Joseph's life, and parish records show him to have served as a churchwarden for three years between 1659 and 1661. In 1674, in his capacity as 'We His Majestie's Justice of the Peace', he also signed the Exemption Certificate for the Hearth Tax.

He gave generously to the community and appears to have shown special interest in the education and training of poor boys, both in Twickenham and in his Manor of Downton, where he founded a school. The Twickenham vestry acknowledged the sum of £10 'to put out poor boys to prentice', and in his will Sir Joseph left '£50 to the poor of the Parish of Twickenham chiefly to put out children to be prentices'. The vestry were greatly appreciative of Sir Joseph's generosity, and in the minutes of 6 September 1670, it was ordered 'that the Churchwardens waite upon Sr Joseph Ashe and return him thanks in the name of the Parish, for two silver flaggons which he gave them for the use of the Communion table'.

The next eighty years were to bring a close connection between the Ashe family and the Felbrigg estate in Norfolk, home of the Windham family and now a National Trust property.

CHAPTER 4

THE FELBRIGG, NORFOLK CONNECTION

The summer of 1669 saw the marriage of Katherine, eldest daughter of Sir Joseph and Lady Ashe, to a wealthy young landowner from Norfolk, William Windham. At seventeen, Katherine was described as 'a gay, generous and warm-hearted girl, later to be a devoted wife and a loving but thoroughly sensible mother to a large family'. She took a generous 'portion' (financial settlement) to the marriage, which was to prove happy and successful, with the birth of eleven children, eight of whom survived to maturity – no mean achievement in the seventeenth century.

William Windham had recently inherited the family estates at Felbrigg in Norfolk, and at twenty-two was already showing a good head for estate management. A deep mutual respect developed between Sir Joseph and William, who benefited greatly from his father-in-law's wisdom and experience in business matters. In 1679, Sir Joseph offered to vacate his seat as Member of Parliament for Downton in order to promote William in a political future, but the borough was adamant against electing strangers.

The young Windhams, although deeply involved in their life at Felbrigg, undertook the arduous journey from Norfolk to Twickenham each year to spend time with Sir Joseph and Lady Ashe, despite Katherine's almost annual pregnancies. (One child, Thomas, was born in a coach outside Bishop's Stortford, but proved to be weak and only survived for two years.) Two of their children were born at Twickenham, where they were baptised in the names of their grandparents: Mary in September 1677 and Joseph (who was later to become the owner of the Twickenham house and lands) in August 1683.

The Ashe connection with Norfolk was strengthened with the marriage in 1673 of Sir Joseph's second daughter, twenty-year-old Mary, to Sir Horatio Townshend, Bt. of Raynham (created 1st Viscount Townshend in 1682), to whom she took a portion of '£8,000

Oil painting on canvas of Katherine Ashe, Mrs William Windham I (1652–1729) by Sir Peter Lely (1618–1680) and studio, c.1669. Lely took the pose from a portrait of Mary of Modena he had painted shortly after her marriage to James II, Duke of York, in 1673, changing only the head. (©National Trust Images/ John Hammond)

with her and a snip of 1500 guineas from the Mama'. Sir Horatio Townshend, a childless widower of forty-two, was a neighbour and friend of William and Katherine Windham. Within eighteen months, Mary gave birth to an heir, baptised Charles in honour of the King, his godfather.

Two more sons were born of the marriage before Mary's untimely death of smallpox in 1685. Her husband survived her for two years, leaving their three sons orphaned.

The eldest, Charles, was educated at Eton with his cousins Ashe and William Windham and their grandparents' house at Twickenham became a convenient place for holidays for all three children, also providing companionship for their young uncle James Ashe, with whom they were of similar age. (Both Katherine and Mary had given birth to sons within a year of the birth of their baby brother.) James led a lonely childhood, with elderly parents and only two maiden sisters for company, each of them more than fifteen years his senior, and incapacitated – Martha was blind and Anne suffered from mental health issues, to use the modern term.

The future of the young Charles Townshend, the 2nd Viscount (later a prominent Whig politician closely associated with Robert Walpole), was a matter of concern to his family. Both Windhams and Ashes made it their business to win the boy's confidence and affection.

The families remained close, and even after he rose to great eminence, Charles Townshend (who earned the nickname of 'Turnip' Townshend in connection with his agricultural reform policy) remained a good friend to his relations. He married twice, the second time in 1713 to Robert Walpole's sister, Dorothy, thus becoming an uncle by marriage to Horace Walpole.

Sir Joseph Ashe, his grandfather, remained active in business until the end of his life, and served as President of the East India Company in 1684–1685. He died at his house in Twickenham on 15 April 1686, and the vestry ordered 'that in regard the Worshipfull Sr Joseph Ashe Bart hath been a great Benefactor to this Parish that a Vault be made in the South Isle of Twickenham Church as near to my lady Bartlett's Vault as may be and the Vaulte to contain seaven feete square'.

A handsome monument, attributed to Grinling Gibbons, was placed in Twickenham Church and can be seen today in the bell tower (see Appendix C).

By his will of 17 March 1685, Sir Joseph bequeathed 'to my deare and beloved wife Dame Mary Ashe All my Mannors Lands Tenements and hereditaments … absolutely … and with the trust and confidence I have in her to give or convey the property to my sonne James or any of my children'. He appointed his widow sole guardian of James, instructing her to pay him 'the Annuall sum of One hundred pounds till he is 16 years of age and Two hundred and fifty pounds afterwards'. He also left his unmarried daughters Martha and Anne the sum of £7,000 each. The following year, a schedule was added to the will, in which Sir Joseph gave £100 to each of his sons-in-law, William Windham and Lord Townshend, 'for mourning', and after various bequests, a sum of £2,000 'to be distributed amongst poor relations'.

Sir James Ashe, owner, 1686–1733

James Ashe succeeded to the Baronetcy at the age of twelve and he, his mother and sisters Martha and Anne remained in the house. As he grew up, Sir James was regarded as 'a very feeble son', and differences arose between him and his mother, who was of a forceful nature. He disobliged her 'by his perverseness to mee, and crossnesse in not marrying where I desired'. Whom Lady Ashe wished her son to marry may never be known, but the marriage that he did contract some time in the 1690s with Catherine Bowyer, the daughter and co-heiress of Sir Edmund Bowyer of Camberwell, was to end in failure.

Lady Ashe abided by the 'trust and confidence' placed in her by her late husband and it would appear that she admitted her son to the Twickenham estate in 1698. A pencilled note in the margin of the Court Rolls for 1657 reads 'L(ad)y Ashe and Mr. James … messuage … and 63a1/2 land 20 October 1698'.

By 1700, Sir James was also taking responsibility for the Downton estate. Lady Ashe had continued the management after her husband's death and correspondence between her and Mr Snow the steward continued from 1686 until 1700, when the first letters are written by Sir James. On 11 February 1700, he wrote to Snow, 'I hope that you are as frugall as may be in expenses for everything grows very dear.'

While Lady Ashe and her daughters remained in the house at Twickenham, Sir James and his wife chose to live in London. A letter sent to Downton on 20 October 1701 requested the sending of '20lbs weight butter pots to Sir James house in Bedford Row near Grey Inn'.

Lady Mary Ashe died on 28 November 1705, having taken infinite pains to ensure that none of her personal fortune should find its way into her son's hands. After her death, Sir James and his wife and their surviving daughters moved into the house at Twickenham, his elder sisters having removed themselves to a house at Whitton.

The Ashe son and heir, Joseph, had died in 1703; a second child, Catherine, died in 1705, and the marriage was disintegrating fast. In 1706–1707, Lady Catherine Ashe was persuaded by her half-brother Sir John Cropley to leave her husband.

A vivid description of the event exists in the curiously mis-spelt but wholly delightful correspondence of Lady Isabella Wentworth, a resident of Twickenham:

> 'it seems Sr Jamse transgressed and went astray, which inraged her soe much that ever senc her last childe, which was thre quarters old she never beded with him never man humbled himself more than he did to her made her all the fair promisis immagenable and to plees her was fflacksed although the Dockters said thear was noe reason for it and the Blynde Sister offered her five hundred pounds att the Birth of her next childe to doe what she would with, but nothing could parswade her soe he saide if she would not bed with him she should not liv with him soe last thursday she went away his coach and six carryed her to the water Syde and her Brothers coach and fower … and the Bigist girl cryed the other twoe are little as she went into the coach but she shed not a tear he has never a son he gave her a purs with five pound pieces and ginneys in it and last Sunday be brought his little girl to Church with him and showed aboundenc of ffondness to it, and it is sade Docter Williams made the sarment for him his tex was if he will goe lett him.'

Shortly after the departure of their mother (who died in 1717, never having returned to Twickenham), the two younger sisters died, leaving Martha, the little girl who cried to see her mother leave, alone with her father.

Sir James Ashe appears to have been an extremely difficult man and, unlike his father, took little or no part in local affairs. In 1713, the Vicar nominated him churchwarden, an office he apparently declined, and his place was filled by Thos. Vernon of Twickenham Parke. There is a reference to Sir James in the vestry minutes for 25 April 1713, when he was appointed one of twenty trustees to consider the rebuilding of the parish church, the nave having collapsed on the night of 9 April 1713. A fund for rebuilding was opened under the direction of Sir Godfrey Kneller, the Court painter, who was a churchwarden of St Mary's. In May of that year, Lady Wentworth wrote, 'I hear Sir Jamse Ashe has geven a hundred pd, his daughter that is but fowerteen has given three scoar, his blind sister a hundred …'

Katherine Windham, a vigorous lady now in her early sixties, travelled occasionally from Norfolk to Twickenham to visit her family, especially her blind sister Martha. Her sister Anne was proving a problem to Martha, as Lady Wentworth wrote: 'Her sister the Mad one sets at her Windoe, and cals al people namse as they com in soe we was carryed a back way and she gives the beger wemen mony to drown all thear Girls she ses thear is soe many wemen in the world and soe few men.' Martha died in August 1714 and was interred in the family vault, but as there is no record of either Anne's death or burial, it is assumed that she was committed to an asylum following the death of her sister.

Katherine Windham was then a widow of some twenty years' standing. Warm-hearted and affectionate, she took pity on her young niece leading a lonely life in the great mansion at Twickenham with her father, and took her back to Norfolk. It was not long before Martha and her cousin Joseph, Katherine's third surviving son, announced their intention of marrying. Martha was barely sixteen or seventeen years old and sole heiress to a large fortune, and Joseph was in his early thirties. Possibly the marriage had been engineered by Katherine Windham in order to retain the house and fortune within the family.

Sir James strongly opposed the match between his daughter and his nephew (who was only nine years younger than Sir James himself) and for some time refused to meet Joseph. Happily, Martha remained devoted to Katherine until her death in 1729, speaking of her aunt and mother-in-law as 'sensible and sweet-tempered'.

Martha and Joseph were married in 1715, but with a gap in the parish registers for that year, it is not clear whether the marriage took place in Twickenham with the blessing of Sir James. Three children were born to the couple, a son, William, who died, and two daughters, Mary and Katherine.

There may have been a reconciliation between father and daughter but, awkward to the end, Sir James died intestate in November 1733, so his intentions regarding the disposal of his estate are not known. Letters of administration were granted to Martha, 'the wife of Joseph Windham and natural and law-full [sic] daughter of Sir James Ashe Bart of Twittenham in the County of Middlesex Widower'.

By a deed dated July 1734, Martha transferred the estate in its entirety to her husband, who adopted the surname of Ashe, and as Joseph Windham Ashe he became not only master of the estate at Twickenham, but also Member of Parliament for Downton in Wiltshire.

Joseph Windham Ashe, owner, 1734–1746

At the time of his marriage to Martha Ashe, Joseph Windham was a wholesale linen draper in Austin Friars. Regarded as a 'man of business' by the family, he acted as a London 'clearing house' and looked after the financial affairs of those who lived in the country or whose duties took them abroad.

The year of 1720, however, saw a drastic drop in the family fortunes. Most members had succumbed to the prevailing hysteria and plunged rather recklessly into investing in the South Sea Company. Joseph, his brothers William and James, and his mother, buying not only for herself but for her eldest son, bought shares lavishly, even using their influence with Lord Townshend and Robert Walpole in order to do so. By the end of the summer, however, the 'South Sea Bubble' had burst, and the value of their stocks plummeted. Joseph lost a great deal of money, as did the rest of the family, but his younger brother James faced financial ruin, losing more than £20,000, and he returned to the Navy, relinquishing his 'comfortable little post' at the Office of the Commissioners of the Duties upon Salt. In 1721, Joseph Windham succeeded to his brother's place in the Salt Office, due to the influence of Robert Walpole. No money was forthcoming from his difficult and cantankerous father-in-law, and Joseph and Martha Windham struggled financially for the next decade, until the death in 1733 of Sir James and Martha's inheritance of her fortune.

In 1734, Joseph and Martha Windham Ashe took possession of the house at Twickenham, and in that same year their daughter Mary married her cousin John Windham, son of Joseph's elder brother William, continuing the strong link between the Ashe and Windham families. The young couple lived at Twickenham with Joseph and Martha, and had six children, born between 1737 and 1745. With his new wealth, Joseph Windham Ashe 'greatly enlarged the house and built the West front' and it was at that time that he built the large orangery to the south of the house, which appears for the first time in a painting by Antonio Joli of 1745 (see Chapter 1). It was an impressive building, surmounted by a cupola, and may have been inspired by the orangery built by his brother at the family home at Felbrigg.

Joseph was certainly not the astute businessman he was considered to be, and it is known that in earlier days his mother had cause to be dissatisfied with his handling of her money affairs. The extent of his alterations to the house proved costly and his lifestyle may have become somewhat extravagant, for he found himself in severe financial difficulties, despite having come into 'an Estate of £4,000 per annum and a great Sum of money'. The extensive and wealthy estate created over thirty years by Sir Joseph Ashe, and carefully maintained by Sir James Ashe for the next fifty, was squandered away in eight short years. On 21 April 1742, he was forced to mortgage the estate, house and grounds, together with 105 acres of lands in the parish (see Appendix A) to one Valens Comyn, to raise the sum of £36,000.. Joseph Windham Ashe died four years later in 1746, aged sixty-three. By his will, he bequeathed all his real and personal estate to his son-in-law John Windham, appointing him sole executor and residuary legatee. John Windham later inherited Bowyer property through his mother-in-law, Martha Windham Ashe, and assumed the name of Windham-Bowyer.

The large mortgage was, however, still outstanding, and by a forfeited conditional surrender of 30 September 1747, the estate now passed to Valens Comyn. A sharp accountant with a distinguished career, he was nonetheless in this period profiting hugely from backing 'privateer' (pirate) raids in the Caribbean. Among his less risky ventures perhaps, Comyn was also credited with drawing up life assurance tables based on life expectancy.

For the next two years, however, the widowed Martha was allowed to remain in the house and her name appears in the poor rate book for July 1748 as paying £8.16s.0d. for the house, plus £1.0s.0d for Ferry Mead. Martha died in 1749, whereupon Valens Comyn took over occupation; the entry for 1749 reads 'Madame Ashe now Mr. Cummins'. The same 'Mr. Cummins' appears in the entries for 1750 and 1751. (Cummins appears to be a misspelling by the clerk for 'Comyn'.)

After assuming control of the Ashe lands, Valens Comyn disposed of two parcels of land to his neighbours (see Appendix B). On 9 October 1747, he sold to George Morton Pitt of Orleans House, six acres of land in Bakers Orchard Close (now the site of Orleans Park School). Seven and one-third acres in Short Farthingworth Close (on the corner of Richmond Road and Montpelier Row) were then sold on 13 April 1748 to the Countess of Suffolk, who was expanding her estate at Marble Hill.

Valens Comyn died intestate in May 1751 and the estate passed to his family. Richard Owen Cambridge was at that time contemplating a move to Twickenham. By an indenture dated 31 December 1751 between 'James Comyn eldest son and heir-at-law (of Valens Comyn since deceased) Richard Comyn and Jane Comyn Spinster daughter and Administratrix, John Windham Bowyer and Mary Catherine Windham ... Richard Owen Cambridge and Mary Cambridge, and Charles Yorke and Robert Kingscote (as Trustees of the Cambridge Family Settlement) the messuage, barns, stables, pigeonhouse, buildings, orchards and gardens near a place called Richmond Ferry; 50 acres of copyhold land in Warren Close adjoining; 12 acres in Long and Short Sandborough Closes; and the close known as Ten Acres' became the property of Richard Owen Cambridge.

With this transaction, the boundaries of the estate to be known as Cambridge Park were formed. Those boundaries remained largely intact until the estate was divided in the 1830s.

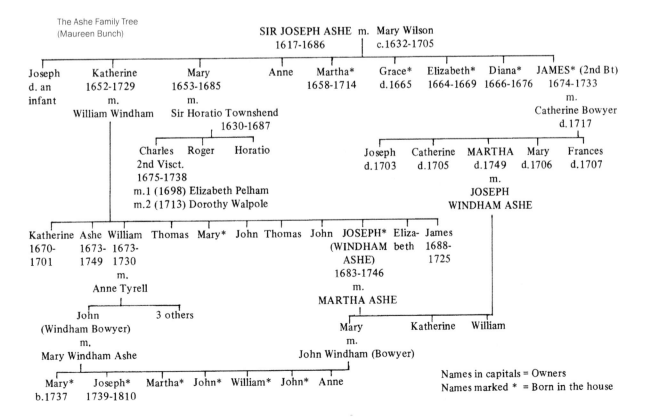

The Ashe Family Tree
(Maureen Bunch)

CHAPTER 5
THE MYSTERY OF THE GLASS HOUSE

John Rocque's map published between 1741 and 1745 shows a property beside the River Thames at Twickenham prominently labelled The Glass House, which appears to consist of a number of buildings. It is not clear why this property was named in preference to the various important estates in the immediate neighbourhood such as Ham House, Orleans House, Marble Hill or Cambridge Park. The land now forms part of Marble Hill Park, at its south-east corner, on the southerly edge of the Cambridge Park estate.

This chapter benefits largely from the scholarship of Twickenham Museum, who identified the earliest reference to this property as an entry in the parish rating assessment of 1652, showing it in the ownership of Sergeant Edward Birkhead, who was behind with his payment of 4/- for 'ye glasse house'. In 1656, John Clarke was paying rent of 2/-. In the 1661 Survey of the Parish, it was still in the ownership of Birkhead and described as 'The Glasse house that Trotts lives in' (James Trott had been listed as a churchwarden in 1643). It was valued at £6, a sum indicating that it was more extensive than a mere cottage.

Later occupiers of this property include a Mr Bright from 1674 to 1677 and Richard Watkins in 1675.

At a vestry meeting of 15 February 1674–1675, it was 'ordered that Mr Billinghurst doe draw Covenants for ye undertakers of ye glassehouse & a bond of £1000 to make good ye covenants & that ye officers be careful to see ye deeds sealed'. Mr Billinghurst's name occurs elsewhere and he appears to have been a lawyer, recorded as living in Whitton between 1672 and 1679. Another reference, in the churchwardens' accounts for 1675 reads: 'paid to John Rogers for going to London to ye masters of ye glasse howse to give in [?security], 4/-'. This may have been the Worshipful Company of Glass Sellers.

The property may at around this time have come into the hands of Robert Bartlett, believed to have been baptised on 10 August 1651, and described as a tallow chandler of Southwark. His widow Sarah inherited land in the immediate area on his death in 1719.

Depicted as three buildings, the property is described as 'The Hatters' on a plan ('Scatch of the Grounds at Twittinhame ...') drawn by John Erskine, the Earl of Mar, in 1711. This description has not been explained: it may refer to the owner or use of part of the property.

Detail from the John Rocque map of 1741-1745 noting The Glass House on the banks of the Thames, next to the Cambridge estate. This area now lies in the south-eastern corner of Marble Hill Park. Curiously, there is little detail other than the name of this 'house' in the whole of the Cambridge Park estate – not even Twickenham Meadows (later Cambridge House) is named. (Image from Twickenham Museum)

Mar (1675–1732) was an enthusiastic amateur architect: he produced drawings of the grounds of Orleans House, belonging to former Secretary of State for Scotland James Johnston (1643–1737), and of Ham House in 1711. These included projects for development, in particular for a house on the site later occupied by Marble Hill House. In 1721, exiled in Paris following his leading role in the failed Jacobite rebellion of 1715, he drew up plans for a quite radical embellishment of Johnston's house. He may also have been responsible for the enlargement of Sir Thomas Skipwith's house further upstream on Twickenham riverside, on the site of the later Poulett Lodge, and the modern-day Thames Eyot development.

In the Rocque map of the 1740s, the original three buildings of the 'Hatters' site have now become four, with the addition of The Glass House, although as the text is added to the east of these, it is likely that this term refers only to this fourth and most recent building.

References to later occupiers, or proprietors, of The Glass House include a Widow Lane in 1718 and 1720, a Mr Swain between 1725 and 1734, and William Plomer, a linen draper, in 1738. Plomer was a son-in-law of Sarah Bartlett; he died in 1747. In 1748, there is a reference to a Mr [?William] Toothacre. Mrs Toothacre was noted for 1749 and she may have been the widow of William, buried on 16 October that year.

In about 1750, the Glass House buildings were probably rebuilt as two smaller houses. One of these was occupied around 1757 by John Fridenberg, a neighbour of the Countess of Suffolk, and who was ejected following a dispute about access. The other was later named as Little Marble Hill, set back from the river on the eastern side of what is now Marble Hill Park.

Evidence for the existence (and duration) of a glass-making works is circumstantial, although the term Glass House was normally used to describe a glass-making factory. The manor court books do not note such a business here although there are references to land described as the 'Glass House Mead'. The property may have been enfranchised as freehold, acquired by the Countess of Suffolk through the agency of the Earl of Islay who was instrumental in putting together the land for the Marble Hill Estate from 1724.

Such a site, well away from other buildings, would have met concerns over the fire hazard and smoke pollution associated with glass manufacturing. In London, there was at the time an Act preventing glass houses from operating within a mile of the Palace of Whitehall. The Glass Excise Act of 1745 penalised the manufacture of heavy glassware, imposing a levy of 9/4d per Cwt (112 lbs) of ordinary glass and 2/4d on each Cwt of green bottle glass. The Act was very unpopular, leading to the licensing of each Glass house for an annual fee of £10 by 1784. The glass excise was finally abolished in 1845.

According to John Serle's *A Plan of Mr. Pope's Garden* of 1745, the tunnel of the grotto linking the house to the garden held 'several Pieces of well-chosen things from the Glass-House'. In the rear chamber, he also described 'Cinders, from the Glass-houses, Furnaces, &c...' The Marble Hill grotto also features coloured glass, possibly from a local source.

The mystery of the Glass House buildings and their true purpose waits to be revealed.

CHAPTER 6

'CAMBRIDGE, THE EVERYTHING'

T he fine Jacobean mansion by Richmond Bridge was eventually named for its most illustrious resident, Richard Owen Cambridge, poet, wit and gentleman of letters, who lived there from 1751 until his death in 1802. During his lifetime, however, the property was still known as 'Twickenham Meadows' and it was only once it had passed out of the Cambridge family's ownership in 1835 that the name of 'Cambridge House' was assumed.

Richard Cambridge was born on 14 February 1717, the only child of Nathaniel Cambridge and Meriel Owen. His father, 'bred into the business of foreign trade as a Turkey merchant', came from a long-established Gloucestershire family, and shortly after the birth of their son in London, Nathaniel and Meriel Cambridge moved to Whitminster House at Wheatenhurst in Gloucestershire.

Richard Owen Cambridge (1717–1802). Engraving by Charles Bestland from the painting by Ozias Humphry, R A.
(© National Portrait Gallery, London)

Ozias Humphry R.A. pinx.   *C. Bestland sculp.*

RICHARD OWEN   *CAMBRIDGE, ESQ.*

ÆT.   SV. LXI.

Nathaniel Cambridge died between 1725 and 1726, and his widow's brother, Thomas Owen, a retired lawyer of considerable means, and childless, assumed responsibility for Richard, adopting him as his heir and supervising his education.

Young Richard attended Eton, where he was viewed as a more or less indifferent scholar, although he showed a deep interest in drama. Many of his contemporaries at the college were to become famous – Prime Ministers Bute, Pitt and Grenville; Lord Chancellors Bathurst and Pratt; and, on the literary scene, Thomas Gray and Horace Walpole. Horace Walpole was in later years to move to Strawberry Hill, Twickenham, where his friendship with Richard Owen Cambridge was renewed.

In 1734, Richard Cambridge entered St John's College, Oxford, as a gentleman commoner, but failed again to distinguish himself as a scholar. He became restless with Oxford and elected to leave without taking a degree, expressing the desire to enter Lincoln's Inn. He moved to London and was admitted to the Inn in 1737, where 'his studies were but languid', and found himself once more in the company of his friends from Eton.

Portrait of Catherine (Mary) (c.1716–1806), wife of Richard Owen Cambridge. Attributed to Ozias Humphry, R A. (© Sotheby's 2021)

In the established eighteenth-century tradition of a young gentleman of means, Richard Cambridge laid out his plans for a Grand Tour, but the severe winter of 1739 to 1740 delayed all possibility of travel. All such schemes, however, were soon forgotten after falling in love with Mary Trenchard, the twenty-three-year-old daughter of George Trenchard, MP for Poole in Dorset, and granddaughter of Sir John Trenchard, Secretary of State to King William III.

Their marriage in the summer of 1740 laid 'the foundation of a most sincere and affectionate attachment that lasted for sixty years' and as an elderly gentleman, Mr Cambridge remarked, 'there is no sight so pleasing to me as seeing Mrs. Cambridge enter a room; and that after having been married to her for forty years.'

After their marriage, the couple settled at the family home at Whitminster, and their first two children were born; Richard in December 1741 and Charlotte in 1746.

At Whitminster, Mr Cambridge led the life of a 'country gentleman whose tastes lay rather in letters and landscape-gardening than farming or field sports'. He disliked guns and took to shooting instead with a bow and arrow, a sport at which he came adept, the head of a duck on the river being a favourite target. Here too he indulged his passion for boats, to the extent of diverting three miles of the River Stroud to lead past his land. On this stream he operated a strange flotilla of boats, among them a twelve-oared barge manned by servants from the estate and various villagers, although the pride of his fleet was probably a craft of his own design, in the style of a Venetian state barge, with a cabin large enough to take thirty people. It was 'handsomely fitted up, and contained in the pannels [sic] between the windows eight pictures painted for the purpose by that eminent marine painter Mr. Samuel Scott, representing every different short of ship, vessel and boat then in use'.

Aboard this boat, Mr Cambridge received Frederick, Prince of Wales, and the Princess, and a large party who were at that time staying with his friend Lord Bathurst at Cirencester. Dinner was served, prepared in a boat tied alongside to serve as a kitchen, and afterwards Mr Cambridge was gratified to receive a letter from Lord Bathurst '... My Royal guests have gone this afternoon and they have charged me with their compliments to you ... they were highly pleased with you and your entertainment and it proved ... the most agreeable day they had passed in their whole progress'.

In January 1748, Richard Cambridge's uncle and guardian Thomas Owen died, leaving the residue of his estate to his nephew, including several properties in London, and lands in Herefordshire and Radnorshire. His will concluded with the request that 'my nephew shall immediately upon my decease assume ... the Sirname [sic] of Owen and in all deeds etc stile and call himself by the Sirname of Owen ... and carry the Coat of Arms ... belonging to the family Owen'.

Following the death of his uncle and the acquisition of not only a new name but a substantial fortune which relieved him of any financial worries for the rest of his life, Richard Owen Cambridge moved his wife and family to a house in London, where they spent the next two years. Here their second daughter Catherine was born in 1750, but the London air disagreed with Mrs Cambridge's health, and the decision was taken to return to the country. Their choice fell on Twickenham where 'the climate has always been celebrated for its pure and healthy influence. The wind blowing from the south or west brings glorious air from the high heath-commons of Hampshire and Surrey', and in 1751, Richard Owen Cambridge took possession of the house by Richmond Ferry where he was to spend the remainder of his life. At Twickenham, their last two sons were born, and baptised at St Mary's Church, Charles in April 1754 and George in August 1756.

Soon after his arrival in Twickenham, Richard Owen Cambridge published his first and major work *The Scribleriad*, a lengthy and satirical mock-heroic poem, which was published in six parts at a cost of 1s. each. Reception of this work was mixed: praised by friends in his own large circle, but not otherwise widely acclaimed. In the following years, several more poems were published, including in 1756, 'An Elegy Written in an Empty Assembly Room' (which drew praise from Horace Walpole) and 'The Fakeer'.

Richard Owen Cambridge was a major contributor to *The World*, a periodical in the *Tatler* tradition, and his witty offerings were well received. Many famous names featured among the contributors (although the papers were always unsigned), including Lord Chesterfield, Horace Walpole and Edward Moore.

A favourite anecdote connected with this venture concerns a sudden appeal by Mr Moore for a story. The note was handed to Mr Cambridge on his way to church one Sunday morning. Noticing his inattention to the sermon, Mrs Cambridge whispered to him, 'What are you thinking of?' He replied 'Of the next "World", my dear.'

Within a short time Mr Cambridge had established himself as a leading member of Twickenham society. Horace Walpole wrote in July 1755: 'We shall be as celebrated as Baiae or Tivoli and, if we have not such sonorous names as they boast, we have very famous people: Clive and Pritchard, the actresses: Scott and Hudson, the painters: my Lady Suffolk (famous in her time as "Mrs. Howard" of Pope and Gay): Mr. Hickey the impudent lawyer: Whitehead the poet: and Cambridge, the everything.'

'Cambridge, the everything' was indeed a worthy epithet for the man. His interests and accomplishments were many and varied, including a flair for landscape gardening. With the mood of eighteenth-century gardening moving towards open aspects and pastoral idylls, the formal gardens that had fronted the house during the tenure of Sir Joseph Ashe underwent drastic change under the supervision of Mr Cambridge.

The Scribleriad by Richard Owen Cambridge. Later republished in *The Works of Richard Owen Cambridge, Esq.* by his son, Archdeacon Cambridge.

High walls and terraces had previously excluded the view of the river, and the grounds were 'so crowded and disfigured by numerous avenues' that the aspect

THE

SCRIBLERIAD:

AN

HEROIC POEM.

BOOK I.

By R.O. Cambridge.

LONDON:
Printed for R. Dodsley in *Pall-mall*;
And Sold by
M. Cooper in *Pater-noster-row.*

M DCC LI.

The Seat of R.ᵒ Owen Cambridge Esq.ᶠᵉ at Twickenham Mid.ˣˣ
Publish'd by I.Sewell Cornhill.

was gloomy and cheerless, in complete contrast with his own nature. He cleared away the walls and hedges in order to open up vistas, and built a grove along the upper part of the meadows about three-quarters of a mile in length, covered in soft turf and bordered with rose bushes, honeysuckle, lilacs and sweet williams, shaded by tall trees and with views through to the meadows where oxen grazed, and beyond to the river and Richmond Hill.

The Seat of Richard Owen Cambridge Esq., showing Cambridge House and Richmond Bridge over the Thames (Richmond upon Thames Local Studies Library and Archive)

For these alterations he received flattering compliments from the famous Lancelot 'Capability' Brown, the great landscape gardener of the day. Mrs Henrietta Pye, writing in 1755, claimed extravagantly:

> 'This Kingdom is situated on the Banks of the Thames: the whole Place is one continued Garden. Plenty and Pleasure are the Ideas conveyed by its large Fields of Corn and its verdant Meadows: 'tis govern'd by a King … his Palace stands in a large Plain, near the Place for embarking, which is the Boundary of his Kingdom … his first Care was to destroy the Palace Gardens: he leaves the Enjoyment of his Meadows and Groves, to his Subjects, which has much encreas'd his Popularity, and has also put up many Seats and Benches, for the Ease and Satisfaction of his people, whose Esteem he makes it his Study to acquire.'

Mr Cambridge's benevolence in throwing open his grounds as a promenade and picnic ground was widely applauded. 'In these delightful meadows, in the summer season, it was customary for parties of pleasure, chiefly Citizens of London, to go up with the tide to the extensive lawn in front of the house, carrying with them a cold repast, and at a proper distance they spread their cloth on the verdant carpet.'

Sadly, in later years, a less welcome crowd began to take its ease by the river and 'the lawns before the house continually exhibited scenes of riot and disorder, whilst the more retiring parts of the garden and grounds, invaded without scruple in open defiance of the proprietor and his servants, became a haunt of the grossest licentiousness and indecency', forcing Mr Cambridge to place notices along the river frontage now forbidding the landing of boats.

Being a man of considerable wit, great conversational powers, and good literary taste, Mr Cambridge's house was the resort of many prominent men of the day: Lord Hardwicke, Lord North (Prime Minister to George III) and Lords Hyde, Gray and Fox; Admiral Boscawen, Lord Anson and Sir Joseph Banks – all were amongst his friends. Other visitors included Captain Cook before his last voyage, James Bruce on his return from Abyssinia, and Captain Vancouver. He never stinted on hospitality, although he did not himself indulge in wine – *'Cantabrigius drinks nothing but water'* wrote Lord Chesterfield.

James Boswell, receiving an invitation to dine at Mr Cambridge's house in the company of Sir Joshua Reynolds and Dr Samuel Johnson, deemed it important enough to cancel a proposed visit to Lord Pembroke at Wilton, for he thought it 'a scene not to be lost'. His diary for 18 April 1775 records: '... *to dine with Mr. Cambridge at his delightful seat on the banks of the Thames at Twickenham ... an elegant entertainment, a very accomplished family, and much good company (which included Mr. James Harris and Mr. Gibbon the historian).'*

Boswell was later to write of Mr Cambridge:

> *'If a beautiful villa on the banks of the Thames ... a numerous and excellent library which he accurately knows and reads, a choice collection of pictures, which he understands and relishes, an easy fortune, an amiable family, an extensive circle of friends and acquaintances distinguished by rank, fashion and genius, a literary fame, various, elegant and still increasing, colloquial talents rarely to be found, and with all these means of happiness enjoying, when well advanced in years, health and vigour of body, serenity and animation of mind, do not entitle him to be addressed 'Fortunate Senex', I know not to whom, if any, that expression could with propriety have been used. Long may he live to hear and feel it.'*

Mr Cambridge's collection of pictures was a further example of his good taste. There were a number of important portraits, including one of the Secretary of State, John Thurloe, by Dobson, as well as Mary Davis, a celebrated actor and mistress of Charles II, and a self-portrait by Angelica Kaufmann. *The View [of the Thames] from Richmond Hill* by Peter Tillemans (now in the Government Art Collection) was 'particularly interesting, so near the spot whence it was taken'. The painting of *Twickenham Meadows* by John Webber, the landscape painter who accompanied Captain Cook on his last voyage to the South Seas, was a 'tribute of gratitude for personal kindnesses received in the house.' (See the Landseer engraving in the Introduction.)

Throughout his life, Mr Cambridge showed a lively interest in current affairs, and it was his habit to rise early and ride to London to spend the day with his friends. After such a day, he would return to his family and, with great pleasure, regale them with amusing stories or more serious matters. That he was a gossip, albeit an amiable one, is without doubt.

'There is not so untittle-tattling a village as Twickenham in the island, and if Mr. Cambridge did not gallop the roads for intelligence, I believe the grass would grow in our ears', wrote Horace Walpole to Lady Ossory. 'If I want literature, or news, yonder is Mr. Cambridge. His friend Mr. Gibbon referred to him as "the Cambridge mail" and David Garrick, another great friend, amused a private gathering with 'a perfect piece of acting … even to the click of encouragement with which one gentleman, inclined to be the hasty bearer of news about a village, would set his horse off again when he had disburdened his mind."'

The imparting of news was indeed a source of great pleasure to Mr Cambridge, but his gossip was never malicious for 'he discovers and diverts himself with the follies of mankind, which his wit enables him to expose with the truest ridicule, although always without personal offence'.

Despite his amiability of character, Mr Cambridge became the subject of a cruel stage caricature, written in vengeful spirit, arising from the matter of the towpath.

During the seventeenth century, barges had been towed by men on the Middlesex bank between Railshead at Isleworth and Twickenham. In 1777, an Act of Parliament was passed empowering the Corporation of London to build a towpath on the Surrey bank, from Kew to Richmond, and to substitute horses for men. A clause was inserted into the Act, however, forbidding the use of horses on the opposite Middlesex bank. This enraged the residents of the riverside houses at Richmond, one of whom was George Colman, a well-known dramatist who ran the Haymarket Theatre.

Suspecting Mr Cambridge of using his friendship with Lord North (then Prime Minister to George III) to influence insertion of the clause to protect the Twickenham path, George Colman launched a literary attack on his rival in the form of a farce entitled *The Manager in Distress*, which he produced at the Haymarket on 20 May 1780. In it, Colman portrayed Mr Cambridge as 'Mr. Bustleton … that idle man of business … who does an infinite deal of nothing because he wants something to do. Talk! … his sentences are periods of a mile … he converses … upon everything; Scandal, Politicks,

Mezzotint print of Horatio (Horace) Walpole, 4th Earl of Orford (1717–1797), friend and near neighbour of Richard Owen Cambridge, through his ownership of Strawberry Hill House (after Sir Joshua Reynolds PRA) by James McArdell (c.1729–1765)
(© National Trust / Kathryn Allen-Kincross)

Religion, Arts, Tabernacles, Theatres, the Court and the Cockpit, Newmarket and the Convocation … he is known by the name of the "Riding Magazine" … he lives a dozen miles out of Town … comes up on a hard trot every day after breakfast, stops every friend he meets to receive and communicate intelligence, and enquires after news from the men of the turnpikes … tells the keeper of the gate at Kensington what he learnt from the toll-gatherer at Hammersmith'.

The play ran for twenty-six nights and was a distinct hit. This satire drew from Horace Walpole the kindest thing he ever had to say about his friend and neighbour. Feeling that Mr Cambridge was unjustly pilloried for his harmless eccentricity, he wrote, 'He had the same right to feel what Colman so resents and he is truly, I mean Cambridge, so benevolent and inoffensive a man, that his little foible does not deserve such treatment.'

Mr Cambridge had indeed, however, played an important part in representing the interests of Twickenham riverside landowners, and was certainly partly, if not wholly, responsible for the inclusion of the clause. Writing to the Earl of Buckingham, the owner of Marble Hill, he said, 'Your Lordship gave me another thing in charge; to watch the Navigation and by no means to relax in what we have obtained by the clause in the Act to have no horses … whatever I have said to prevent horses here I have never proposed (to save our side) to send 'em over to the t'other …'

Although Mr Cambridge was a devout Christian, he does not appear on the list of churchwardens of St Mary's, remaining a member of the congregation, for 'whatever his engagements, he constantly passed Sunday at home with his family, at the head of whom he never failed to attend public service … until prevented by bodily infirmity'. It was his custom to lead family prayers each evening at nine o'clock and on one visit Horace Walpole committed the faux pas of overstaying the hour, but later wrote that 'Old Cherrytree was very good humoured and gracious …' 'Old Cherrytree' was a reference to Mrs Cambridge, towards whom Horace Walpole remained extremely cool, once remarking that 'a Yorkshire Sunday is as prudish as Mrs. Cambridge'.

Neither was Horace Walpole impressed with Mr Cambridge's spinster daughter Charlotte, whom he also considered a gossip. 'She put such a volume of interrogation to me about Lord Stafford's Will. I was forced to say "Madam, I cannot answer all these questions", on which she did close her incessant lips.' He nicknamed her 'Miss Au-près-du-Pont'.

Described as having 'beauty of person, cheerful temper, pleasing manners and a strong constitution', Mrs Cambridge was a constant companion of her husband, accompanying him on horseback in all his active pursuits, although in her latter years she preferred to remain quietly at home. As a result, George Owen Cambridge, the youngest son, took to accompanying his father when visiting the drawing rooms of the 'Blue Stocking' hostesses, among them Mrs Vesey, Mrs Montagu, Lady Egremont and the Duchess of Portland. Mr Cambridge, Horace Walpole and Soame Jenyns, known collectively as 'the Old Wits', were regular visitors, and it was at one of these gatherings that George, a young curate of twenty-seven, first met Frances (Fanny) Burney, the successful young authoress of *Evelina* and *Cecilia*. The attraction appears to have been mutual and it was soon observed that 'Miss Burney has apparently got an admirer in Mr. George Cambridge'.

Mr Cambridge Snr also took an interest in Fanny Burney and on many occasions appropriated her company, which caused comment among the ladies, and soon Miss Burney was visiting the family at

Twickenham, where a deep and lasting friendship developed between her and George's sister, Charlotte. Throughout 1783, meeting constantly, George Owen Cambridge and Fanny Burney's feelings for each other appeared to be deepening, but George, lacking his father's strength of character (or possibly overshadowed by it) never made a declaration. He was a diffident young man, 'very unaffected, pleasant and charming', and a friend of Fanny's wrote '... watching how Mr. George Cambridge pray'd, preached etc ... You would scarcely believe how much more genteelly than well he did both ...'

Bewildered and uncertain, Fanny poured her feelings into diaries and letters. 'I was alive, sufferingly alive to every look – whisper, glance ...' and 'at the well known knock at the door' she would tremble, feel ill and be forced to smell her salts. On happier days, she was 'monopolized either by Mr. Cambridge or his son – by the latter so much the most', but still George never made his feelings known, and by 1786, Fanny, recognising the situation as hopeless, reluctantly accepted a position at Court with Queen Charlotte. Her diaries for 1786 to 1787 show all the bitterness of unrequited love: 'who ... could, or can pardon such wanton, such accumulating – such endless deceit and treachery? I can use no other words; his conduct has long past [sic] all mere impeachment of trifling – it has seemed irrepressibly attached to me – it has been deemed honourably serious by all our mutual acquaintances.'

Frances (Fanny) Burney's early success with *Evelina* was the beginning of a long writing career that produced three more novels, eight plays and multiple volumes of journals and letters. Burney's writing is characterised by sharply delineated characters, a nuanced understanding of the dynamics of social class and complex, multi-threaded plots that weave together many characters. Painting by Edward Francisco Burney (her cousin), oil on canvas, c.1784–1785 (© National Portrait Gallery, London)

In 1793, Fanny married Alexandre d'Arblay, and two years later, George Owen Cambridge married the 'young and beautiful Cornelia van Mierop', thirteen years his junior. George was at that time Rector of Elme in Cambridgeshire, and two years later, was elevated to a Prebendal Stall at Ely Cathedral.

In his declining years, Richard Owen Cambridge's visits to London became less frequent, and he confided to Warren Hastings that 'tho' I love conversation, my Deafness obliges me to take up with Tete a Tete'. Riding down the slope of Richmond Hill one morning, he was met by George III and Lord North, who stopped to converse. The King remarked, 'Mr. Cambridge, you do not ride as fast as you used to.' 'Sir', replied Mr Cambridge, 'I am going downhill.' Not only did his age preclude Mr Cambridge from visiting London, but the local roads were also becoming dangerous at night and 'three coaches ... returning from the play at Richmond were robbed by a squadron of seven footpads close to Mr. Cambridge's at Richmond Bridge.'

For reasons unknown, Richard Owen Cambridge entered into an agreement with the Duke of Montagu in February 1787 for the eventual sale of Cambridge House and the estate for £14,000, the sum of £4,000 to be paid 'in hand' and the balance of £10,000 on the death of Mr Cambridge. In his will made ten years later, Mr Cambridge left to his daughter Charlotte 'the full and compleat sum of £4,000 to be paid out of the Ten thousand pounds due at my death from the Executors of the late Duke of Montagu for compleating the purchase of my estate at Twickenham'. The agreement may have been entered into to ensure the future of his unmarried daughter, but, whatever the intent, the agreement was rescinded on 18 April 1801, at which time Mr Cambridge agreed to repurchase the property from the Duchess of Buccleuch (daughter of the late Duke of Montagu) by repaying the £4,000 'without interest'. However, it 'not being convenient' for Mr Cambridge to repay immediately, a bond was entered into, with George Owen Cambridge standing surety for his father (who was now in his mid-eighties and becoming feeble), with interest charged at five per cent.

Richard Owen Cambridge died at Cambridge House on 17 September 1802, in his eighty-sixth year, survived by his widow, his sons Charles and George, and his daughter Charlotte. His eldest son, also Richard Owen Cambridge, had died many years earlier, leaving a young son, in turn christened Richard Owen Cambridge, who lived with his grandparents at Twickenham. This grandson had sadly died in 1775 at the age of nine and was buried in the family vault at St Mary's, the local parish church. Catherine, his second daughter, had suffered poor health for many years, and had died in June 1784. The second son, Charles, married twice and resided in the family house at Whitminster, where he died in the 1840s.

A tablet to the memory of Richard Owen Cambridge and his family was placed in the gallery at St Mary's Church, beneath that of Alexander Pope's parents (see Appendix C).

By his will dated 15 April 1797, Richard Owen Cambridge appointed his son George as executor, and bequeathed him 'all the live and deadstock … furniture, prints, books and manuscripts in the house at Twickenham', freehold houses in Fleet St, and houses held under Crown Lease in Jermyn St, Market St and St James's. Mrs Cambridge received lands in Gloucestershire, together with 'all plate, jewels, wine, beer and coal at Twickenham', and Charlotte received an annuity of £200 a year.

There is a curious omission from his will of his son Charles Owen Cambridge. Provision was made for him with the house in Gloucestershire (Whitminster, which Mrs Cambridge initially inherited). Charles later became President of the Gloucester General Infirmary, and died in 1847 without heirs.

A codicil was added to the will a few months before Mr Cambridge died, in which Cambridge House and associated lands were unexpectedly left to his maiden daughter, Charlotte.

Mystery surrounds the existence of a third daughter, Mary, to whom Mr Cambridge left an annuity of £160. No records have been discovered of her birth or death, there is no mention of her by other members of the family, and she remains a shadowy figure.

Following Richard Owen Cambridge's death at the start of the nineteenth century, the next hundred years saw a transformation of the estate, and of the greater London area as a whole, that would have been inconceivable during his day.

Richmond Bridge, 1776.

CHAPTER 7
BUILDING RICHMOND BRIDGE

A ferry had been running between Richmond and the Twickenham side of the river since at least the fifteenth century. This had always belonged to the Crown, leased to royal servants or favourites to operate it. It most likely dated back even earlier, to Edward III's building of Shene Palace (renamed as Richmond by Henry VII) in the fourteenth century. Henry VII, VIII and Elizabeth I will all have made use of it. In 1622, it was leased to Edmund Cooke and Edmund Sawyer, granting rights of inheritance. One boat carried passengers and another horses, carts and bulky goods; carriages, however, had to travel via Kingston Bridge.

In the eighteenth century, pressure grew to replace the ferry with a permanent bridge. Both banks of the Thames were increasingly under development, and Horace Walpole was one traveller who documented difficulties in using the ferry, the river sometimes being too swollen for it to cross.

A print of William Hodges' drawing of Richmond Bridge under construction in 1776. Large blocks of Portland stone are shown transported on barges along the river, with one such block hauled up to the deck of the bridge on the right, where a group of four stonemasons are working on the voussoirs of the last arch. (By permission of Richmond upon Thames Borough Art Collection, Orleans House Gallery)

The proposal in the 1770s to replace the ferry at Richmond with a bridge had some impact on Richard Owen Cambridge, who was appointed as one of ninety commissioners to supervise the building of the bridge. Appointed under the Richmond Bridge Act of 1773, the commission included, among others, Lancelot 'Capability' Brown, Horace Walpole, the actor David Garrick, and Sir Charles Asgill, the local MP. Rent at this stage was £3.13s.4d. per year. The lease of the ferry had previously been held by Joseph Windham Ashe, the former owner of Twickenham Meadows, and at his death the lease passed to his nephew, William Windham. The latter's only interest in the ferry was its business potential, and in 1760, he himself had applied for permission to build a bridge across the river.

With twenty-six years still to run, he now offered the ferry lease to the Crown Commissioners, asking for £6,000 but offering to fund a new bridge. He petitioned the House of Commons to bring in a Bill, but was opposed by local residents because his bridge would be privately owned, built of wood, and inconvenient from the Richmond bank (the approach to Ferry Hill – now Bridge Street – was very steep). Opponents suggested instead a stone bridge, from the end of Water Lane, and were backed by the trustees of the Richmond vestry, so Windham withdrew his Bill.

The commissioners purchased Mr Windham's interests and planned for a stone bridge costing £26,000, raising tontine shares of £100 each: each shareholder would receive a share of tolls until death (with the initial annual dividend set at four per cent), following which, their shares would be added to those of the other shareholders. This tontine would continue up to the death of the last shareholder. Many shareholders were consequently listed as children, with the last survivor dying in 1859 at eighty-six, receiving £800 for each of her last five years. Investors had to sign confirmation that they were still alive before receiving the biannual payment.

The bridge commissioners first met in July 1773, and appointed a clerk, who wrote to Lord Frederick Cavendish on 6 September regarding the sale of the necessary Twickenham land. He replied on 17 September from Chatsworth that 'the land does not properly belong to me. The Duchess of Newcastle is in possession and whatever she chooses to do will be agreed by all those who are concerned.'

Disputes continued over the precise siting of the bridge on each bank. On the Surrey side, residents of Water Lane, along with Mr Windham (lessee of the Feathers Inn on the corner with King Street), opposed widening the lane and continuing the road straight into George Street, while everyone else on that side opposed the alternative, steep Ferry Hill approach.

The owner of Twickenham Farm on the Middlesex side, opposite Water Lane, was against the plan: the Duchess of Newcastle, residing in Twickenham Park, and her co-trustees under Lady Mountrath's will, Lord Frederick Cavendish and the Duke of Montrose, as owners of the land, had the final say.

After years of dispute, the Ferry Hill site was finally settled upon by the commissioners, crossing over to Ferry Lane (later known as Richmond Road) on the Twickenham side. Members of the commission were appointed to meet Mr Cambridge to determine the exact limits of the land to be taken from Twickenham Park so that it could be inserted in the conveyance. An agreement was at last laid out before the commissioners in May 1774.

During the construction phase, the right to operate the ferry was now assumed by the commissioners of the bridge, who, finding their income from the ferry tolls endangered by competition from freelance ferrymen, wrote to Mr Cambridge in 1775, requesting him 'to give directions to prevent boats landing upon his meadow which ply for hire from the opposite shore'. Horace Walpole's references to Cambridge as 'Mr Foot of the Bridge' seemed more pertinent than ever.

Richmond Bridge was built between 1774 and 1777 by Thomas Kerr, following a design by James Paine and Kenton Couse. Paine was a leading Palladian architect, seemingly appointed without competition, who later designed three other Thames bridges. Henry Hobart, the leading commissioner, laid the first stone. Money ran out late in the project, so an additional £5,000 was raised in November 1776. The bridge was at last completed and fully opened in December 1777, with pedestrians able to use the crossing from autumn 1776.

An obelisk, still present, was constructed on the Surrey side stating the construction dates and showing mileages to London, Middlesex and Surrey destinations; it also warned that 'Persons who damage or deface the bridge will be prosecuted'. Although slightly widened and its arches flattened in 1937, the bridge is today the oldest surviving construction over the Thames in London. Despite its style and charm, however, its limitations have always constrained public transport services locally, in the form of trams, trains and the Tube.

Richmond Bridge, built in 1774–1777: the viewpoint is from the Richmond side towards East Twickenham. It shows a pair of toll houses, with the keeper collecting their dues from a couple in a gig. On the left is the gate of a boarding house. This picture by James Isaiah Lewis, dated 1890, excluding the dogs added in the foreground and the figures in the centre, is a copy of an engraving by J D Harding, published in *Richmond and its Surrounding Scenery* (1832). (By permission of Richmond upon Thames Borough Art Collection, Orleans House Gallery)

CHAPTER 8
ARCHDEACON CAMBRIDGE THE BENEFACTOR

Following the death of his father in 1802, George Owen Cambridge and his wife, Cornelia, returned to Twickenham, where George assumed control of the estate on behalf of his mother and sister, Charlotte having inherited the house and lands. The widowed Mrs Cambridge survived her husband for four years, dying in 1806 shortly before her ninetieth birthday.

George Owen Cambridge settled back into life in his boyhood home, and occupied himself by editing *The Works of Richard Owen Cambridge, Esq.*, 'including several pieces never before published with an Account of his Life and Character', which was brought out in 1803.

George Owen Cambridge, Archdeacon of Middlesex (1756-1841) (Image from Twickenham Museum)

He became involved in local parochial affairs, and in 1805 purchased the proprietorship for life of Montpelier Chapel, where he officiated 'with a commendable zeal and felicity'. (Montpelier Chapel was a private unconsecrated chapel-of-ease in Chapel Road off Montpelier Row, built in 1727 by Captain John Gray, who had built the first houses in the Row.) The following year saw his appointment as Archdeacon of Middlesex.

George Owen Cambridge had a zeal for charitable work. In the late 1790s, Horace Walpole wrote of contributing £50 to George 'the Infallible' for his potato fund for the poor, and in 1820, he was one of the largest contributors to the Twickenham Bounty Fund, set up after a particularly harsh winter to help the needy. He was also active with the Whitechapel Society for the Education of the Poor.

The youthful friendship between George Owen Cambridge and Fanny Burney (now Mme d'Arblay and widowed) may have reached a bitter conclusion, on Fanny's side at least, but they were to meet again over the years on more friendly terms, and Fanny is known to have visited Cambridge House for a whole fortnight in 1821.

Considered by many to have 'broken Fanny's heart', George was to pay 'handsome recompense in friendship towards that absent-minded, eccentric and hapless young man, Mme. d'Arblay's son …' As Archdeacon of Middlesex, George Owen Cambridge used his influence to enter Alexander d'Arblay into the Church of England and to secure for him a post as curate at a new chapel in Camden Town. At the consecration of the chapel, Fanny d'Arblay was a guest in the vicar's pew, with, 'steadfast beside her, Archdeacon Cambridge'.

Several years later, Archdeacon Cambridge asked Alexander d'Arblay to undertake the ministry of Ely Chapel in Holborn, and Fanny wrote that 'the Archdeacon has been exquisite in judgment, delicacy, wisdom as well as in true kindness'.

Miss Charlotte Cambridge died in March 1823, leaving Cambridge House and lands and all her personal estate to George and Cornelia Cambridge, appointing them both as executors.

The extent of the Cambridge Park estate at the time of her death, measuring 74 acres 1 rood, is shown on the plan attached to the Enclosure Award for Twickenham, 1818, indicated by the numbers 873–881 inclusive.

The island later known as Glover's Island, lying mid-river at the foot of the Old Warren and numbered 881 on the Enclosure Award, left the ownership of the Cambridge family some time between 1818 and 1868.

Three small pieces of land had been added to the estate since the death of Richard Owen Cambridge, when George Owen Cambridge was granted a licence in December 1802 to enclose waste land, comprising 'three several small pieces … All of them situate … on the right hand side of the King's Highway leading from the Town of Twickenham to Richmond Bridge … At the yearly rental of 1s to be paid on the Feast of St. Michael the Archangel in every year.'

Plan attached to the Enclosure Award for Twickenham, 1818

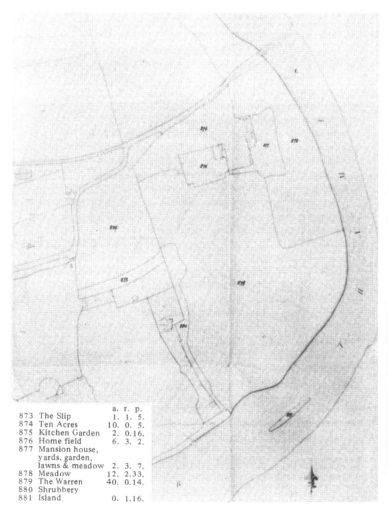

		a.	r.	p.
873	The Slip	1.	1.	5.
874	Ten Acres	10.	0.	5.
875	Kitchen Garden	2.	0.16.	
876	Home field	6.	3.	2.
877	Mansion house, yards, garden, lawns & meadow	2.	3.	7.
878	Meadow	12.	2.33.	
879	The Warren	40.	0.14.	
880	Shrubbery			
881	Island	0.	1.16.	

As part of his good works, Archdeacon Cambridge acted as treasurer for the committee involved in fundraising for a new church, Holy Trinity, on Twickenham Green, for which he laid the foundation stone on 12 August 1840. He did not live to see the completed church, dying in May 1841, aged eighty-five, whereupon he was buried in the family vault at St Mary's Church, Twickenham.

Later, his widow had the trowel used for the foundation ceremony fashioned into a small silver chalice and paten, donating this to the new church. An inscription on the case of the chalice reads as follows:

THIS SACRAMENTAL PLATE

for the private administration

OF THE HOLY COMMUNION

is presented by Mrs Cambridge

TO TRINITY CHURCH on Twickenham Common

being in part formed out of the Silver Trowel

WHICH WAS PRESENTED TO

THE LATE VENERABLE ARCHDEACON CAMBRIDGE

on the occasion of his laying

THE FIRST STONE OF THAT CHURCH

on the 31st of August 1840

The Archdeacon Cambridge Schools on Twickenham Green were built as a memorial to him in 'grateful remembrance of his liberal contribution towards the erection and endowment of the Church of Holy Trinity'. This contribution consisted of the gift of 19 acres of land to the newly created parish. The schools, originally separate infant and junior establishments, were opened in 1842, later received an endowment of £700 from the Archdeacon's widow towards the cost of their maintenance, or the salaries of the teachers.

Before this, however, the Archdeacon's life was to have one final chapter in another fine house on the Middlesex bank of the river, an episode which eventually led to the division of the estate.

MEADOWBANK.

CHAPTER 9
MEADOWBANK AND MEADOWSIDE

Back in 1824, with his fraternal duties finally concluded following his sister's death, Archdeacon Cambridge and his wife were delighted to move to a comfortable home built for them at the southern end of the meadows, on land known as the Old Warren. The new villa, which came to be known as Meadowbank, was certainly a handsome addition along the banks of the river. But this first division of the estate heralded a new phase of redevelopment that would change for ever this leafy stretch of the East Twickenham riverside.

Meadowbank, lithograph by T Scott from the 1877 sale catalogue (Richmond upon Thames Local Studies Library and Archive)

The old family mansion, Cambridge House, was meanwhile leased to Lord Mount Edgcumbe (1764–1839). Minister of Parliament for Fowey in Cornwall, and later member of the Privy Council and Fellow of the Royal Society, Edgcumbe was a celebrated connoisseur of Italian opera, and penned a book on the subject, *Musical Reminiscences of the Earl of Mount Edgcumbe* (1834), still cited by musicologists to this day. In retirement, he was a leading light of amateur theatricals at Strawberry Hill under the author and sculptor Anne Seymour Damer (1748–1828), to whom her godfather Horace Walpole had bequeathed a lifetime interest in his beloved home.

By 1835, the Archdeacon was nearing eighty. Cambridge House was in urgent need of repair and modernisation, and with no children to inherit the estate, the Archdeacon and Mrs Cambridge took the decision to dispose of what they could no longer manage. On 27 February 1835, 'All that copyhold or customary Mansion with yards, barns, stables etc ... being near Richmond Bridge in a field formerly called East Field, together with 30 acres adjoining' was sold to Henry Bevan Esquire for the sum of £6,245.5s.0d. (See Chapter 10).

The Archdeacon himself retained only the remaining 44 acres surrounding his new villa. This historic transaction, dividing the original estate in two, finally led to the demise of the old Cambridge House and Park.

Smaller than Cambridge House, Meadowbank contained at least sixteen rooms on two floors. In addition, the domestic offices consisted of a servants' hall, housekeeper's room, butler's pantry and six staff bedrooms, together with a large kitchen, scullery, various larders and wine cellars. Outside were stables containing six stalls and two loose boxes, three double coach houses, a harness room and rooms above for the grooms, all set around a carriage yard. A separate gardener's cottage was provided, together with vinery and cucumber houses and, well removed from the house, a cow shed. A separate building housed the dairy.

Below: The Lodge on the corner of Alexandra Road in 1910 (Richmond upon Thames Local Studies Library and Archive)

To welcome visitors and their carriages, an entrance and rustic lodge house were constructed at what is now the corner of Cambridge Park and Alexandra Road. 'This picturesque Lodge, shaded by fine elms and adorned with various creeping plants and flowers, is built in the style of some of the rustic cottages in Wales, and is well worth the attention of visitors making a short stay at Richmond.' Engraved by W B Cooke in his *Handbook for Richmond and Twickenham* (1842), it also 'attracted admiration as the subject of a painting in the British Gallery'.

Right: Print of the lodge entrance to Archdeacon Cambridge's grounds by Harding and Cooke from 1832, with figures and cattle in the foreground, showing the rural nature of the estate.
(By permission of Richmond upon Thames Borough Art Collection, Orleans House Gallery)

Drawn by J.D.Harding.   Engraved by W.B.Cooke.

THE LODGE ENTRANCE TO ARCHDEACON CAMBRIDGE'S GROUNDS.

London. Published June 1. 1832. by W.B. Cooke. 22. Charlotte Street. Bloomsbury.

Another entrance was made, together with a lodge, opposite the Rising Sun inn, and the rate book for January 1825 shows the following entry:

> Revd. Archdeacon Cambridge. Mansion, Pleasure grounds, garden, offices and meadows (Cambridge House) valued at £340
>
> Chapel (in Montpelier Row) 30
> Dwelling (Meadow Bank) 60
> Two lodges. 12

Between 1832 and 1833, Archdeacon Cambridge built a second villa on a strip of land alongside his new house, adjoining the boundary with Little Marble Hill (then owned by the Brent family). This villa, 'a substantial house close to Little Marble Hill … lying back from the river', known as Meadowside Cottage, was occupied by Captain Henry Jelf Sharp, a friend of the family.

Following the sale of Cambridge House to Henry Bevan, Archdeacon Cambridge lived on for six years, dying in the spring of 1841 at the age of eighty-five. His estate now passed to his widow Cornelia, with the exception of Meadowside Cottage, which was left in trust to Captain Henry Jelf Sharp until the death of Cornelia Cambridge.

A codicil added shortly before the Archdeacon's death bequeathed further land to Captain Jelf Sharp, again held in trust, consisting of a portion of the meadow between Meadowside Cottage and the river, a strip alongside the boundary of Little Marble Hill known as The Plantation, and the Ten Acre Field bordered by the Richmond Road (see the Warren map of 1846, Nos. 34, 36, 37 and 38).

Captain Jelf Sharp appears to have encountered financial difficulties, and seemingly aware that he would one day inherit Meadowside Cottage outright, began to raise money by a series of mortgages against 'his interest in the remainder expectant on the death of Mrs. Cornelia Cambridge'. In June

Warren's map of 1846 shows the position of the two entrance lodges, at the west end of today's Alexandra Road and opposite the Rising Sun pub. Area B shows the land retained by the Cambridge family, including Meadow Bank. The original carriage driveways within Archdeacon Cambridge's property were followed in the later roads layout in Cambridge Park. Area A defines the land purchased by Henry Bevan to the north, including Cambridge House; some of the estate walls from this period are still in existence.

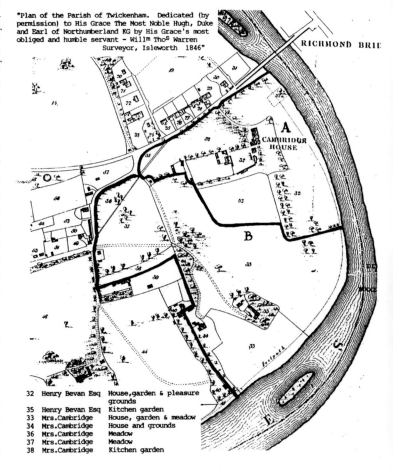

"Plan of the Parish of Twickenham. Dedicated (by permission) to His Grace The Most Noble Hugh, Duke and Earl of Northumberland KG by His Grace's most obliged and humble servant – Willm Thos Warren Surveyor, Isleworth 1846"

32	Henry Bevan Esq	House, garden & pleasure grounds
35	Henry Bevan Esq	Kitchen garden
33	Mrs. Cambridge	House, garden & meadow
34	Mrs. Cambridge	House and grounds
36	Mrs. Cambridge	Meadow
37	Mrs. Cambridge	Meadow
38	Mrs. Cambridge	Kitchen garden

1844, he raised £2,000, with a further £1,000 in April 1847, and in May 1857 he took out yet another mortgage for £5,000, enabling him to clear the two previous arrangements.

In the event, Mrs Cornelia Cambridge, who was many years younger than her late husband, survived the Archdeacon by seventeen years, finally dying at the ripe age of eighty-nine in January 1858. After bequests to her servants, she left £500 to Captain Jelf Sharp, at the same time releasing him from a debt of £350 that had been outstanding for fourteen years. Under a codicil added in 1852, he also received a further £300. The residue of her estate, which included Meadowbank and thirty acres of land, Cornelia Cambridge left to the Reverend Richard William Jelf, Canon of Christ Church, Oxford, and Principal of King's College, London, and his younger brother the Reverend William Edward Jelf, the sons of Sir James Jelf, Kt., of Gloucester. Captain Jelf Sharp had been granted licence to assume the name 'Sharp' following his marriage to Clarissa Amelia Sharp in 1831.

This disposition of the Cambridge estate no doubt results from the long-standing and close friendship between the Cambridge and Jelf families. Both originated in Gloucestershire and the Archdeacon is known to have baptised Richard William Jelf 'privately at Gloucester and publicly in Twickenham parish' in 1798. George Jelf, a barrister, served as the Archdeacon's executor and 'from motives of regard', the Archdeacon had settled the sum of £10,000 on him at the time of Jelf's marriage in 1838.

Upon the death of Mrs Cambridge, Captain (now Major) Jelf Sharp came into absolute ownership of Meadowside Cottage and its adjoining land. The Cambridge estate was now sub-divided into three parts:

Meadowbank, c.1868, from George Bishop's personal photo album (Howard Webb Collection)

'Cambridge House and 30 acres. Mr. Henry Bevan.
Meadowbank and 30 acres. The Revd. R.W. Jelf and Revd. W.E. Jelf.
Meadowside Cottage and 14 acres. Major Jelf Sharp.'

Meadowbank was enfranchised on 5 July 1860, with a fee of £230 paid to the Duke of Northumberland as Lord of the Manor of Isleworth Sion, enabling the Jelf brothers to offer the property for sale as freehold. Cambridge House and Meadowside Cottage remained in copyhold to the Manor of Isleworth Sion.

On 4 January 1861, Meadowbank was now sold to Mr John Parson of Ham Common for £10,000. Mr Parson appears to have been somewhat of a property speculator, judging from his involvement also in the purchase and resale of York House in Twickenham two years later. In the case of Meadowbank, he raised a small mortgage of £3,800, then put his plans in motion. His first move was to enclose the house, together with the surrounding garden and nine acres of land fronting the river. Two months later he sold it for £6,000, at the same time discharging his mortgage. On the 20 acres John Parson had retained, he now set about constructing a new house and grounds, later known as Haversham Grange.

The new owner of Meadowbank, meanwhile, was a wealthy amateur astronomer, George Bishop, who in 1863 erected an observatory in the gardens, using the instruments and dome previously set up at the home of his late father in Regents Park, where city smoke and light pollution had obscured clear views of the night sky. (For more on the observatory and the neighbouring property of Haversham Grange, see Chapter 11). The Cambridge House part of the estate, meanwhile, underwent its own transformation.

CHAPTER 10

THE ESTATE DIVIDED

W hen Henry Bevan (1776–1860) and his wife, Harriet Droz (1783–1852), acquired Cambridge House, it was already more than two hundred years old and in need of a major overhaul. Mr Bevan was exceedingly rich, as member of a family whose fortunes were based on banking and brewing. His father, Silvanus Bevan, was a partner in the banking firm of Barclay – the precursor of today's Barclays Bank, the oldest surviving Quaker bank in London, having been founded in 1690. In 1781, Silvanus Bevan was a sleeping partner in the purchase of a brewery in Southwark from the Thrale family for £135,000, which became the highly successful Barclay, Perkins Brewery; he eventually surrendered his share in that business to his sons Henry and Charles. Henry Bevan was made a partner of the bank early in the nineteenth century.

By 1910, Cambridge House was still beautifully decorated, as shown by the hand-painted wallpaper in this room. (Richmond upon Thames Local Studies Library and Archive)

His considerable wealth enabled him to use the services of Lewis Vulliamy (1791–1871), a fashionable and leading architect of the period, in the extensive alterations he carried out after his purchase of Cambridge House in 1835. Lewis Vulliamy's work was well known in Richmond, where he built the Church of St John the Divine (1830–31), followed by Hickey's Almshouses in 1834. He was also engaged by Sir William Dundas (Sergeant-Surgeon to King William IV) to work on Queensberry House, the building previously on the site of the current twentieth-century apartment development, and in 1852 he constructed St Margarets House for the 2nd Earl of Kilmorey.

No plan survives detailing Vulliamy's work on the house, but from a photograph of 1902, it would appear that two bays running the full height of the building were added at either side of the seventeenth-century flat front facing the river, and that a large conservatory was constructed at the south end of the house.

Cambridge House, decorated for the Coronation of King Edward VII in 1902 (Richmond upon Thames Local Studies Library and Archive)

An article from 1837 in *The Gardener's Magazine*, the first publication of its genre, described this conservatory as:

> 'constructed in superior style … about 40 feet long with a span roof of glass, heightened at the top, by the upper range of lights on each side being raised on an upright range of glass constructed upon the extremity of the lower range, and supported by elliptical and ornamental iron brackets, which give a good relief, and particularly when they are clothed with creepers. This house has a stage in the centre and is well furnished with plants; while, by the assistance of several ornamental devices and a large vase containing gold fishes, it is rendered attractive, and forms a handsome appendage to the drawing room.'

The grounds attached to the house were also the subject of alteration. William Keane, writing in *The Beauties of Middlesex* (1850), was effusive in his praise:

> 'Cambridge House is entered by a handsome lodge-gate from the high road near Richmond Bridge. The approach sweeps through a plantation of trees

and shrubs: these are worthy of particular notice for the taste displayed in their arrangement … each is a distinct and perfect specimen feathered to the greensward. It is a fine exemplification of the gardenesque style of embellishment and produces a beautiful and striking effect. The house, a large commodious building, was enlarged and improved for the present owner by Vulliamy. On the east front is a terrace-walk, 120 yards long, which is adorned in the summer season with large orange trees and beautiful statuary; an undulating velvet lawn rises to a mound on the north-east side and a delightful glimpse of Richmond Bridge is caught through among the trees. When we inform our readers that a broad reach of the majestic Thames and the picturesque villas imbosomed in wood and backed by famed Richmond Hill, are presented to close view, it will easily be conceived that it is rare to find a more distinguished landscape.'

Striking a more practical note, a kitchen garden measuring one and a half acres was formed on the west side of the house. Surrounded and divided by brick walls, the garden was entered through wrought-iron and bronze gates and contained two good ranges of forcing houses together with pits for the growing of pineapples, melons, cucumbers, asparagus, etc. These two forcing houses for the provision of delicate fruits for the dining table totalled 170 feet; the larger, nearly 100 feet long, was divided into three for the growing of early and late peaches, figs and vines.

The Gardener's Magazine advised its readers that these houses were:

> 'constructed in the most substantial manner … without regard to expense. All the houses are heated with hot water, which Mr. Wilson, the gardener, approves of beyond any other system of heating. … On the side of the approach from the kitchen-garden, a lofty span-roofed orangery has been erected; its dimensions are 50 ft. long by 25 ft. wide. The roof is hipped, or sloped back, to the ends and half the roof at the back is of glass and half of slate. The house is warmed with hot water; but, on account of its loftiness, the frost must be with difficulty kept out in severe weather.'

The position of the kitchen garden, greenhouses and orangery is shown in detail on the Ordnance Survey map of 1869 (see next page), to the west and south of Cambridge House. It is likely that this orangery was erected on the site of the earlier orangery built by Joseph Windham Ashe in around 1740.

Today, a high brick garden wall spans the west side of a number of Morley Road gardens, on the west side of the street. A buttress at No. 34 suggests there may have been an adjoining, perpendicular wall running in the direction of today's Cambridge Road and the site of Cambridge House. From No. 36 Morley Road, next door, across the road to No. 41, the foundations of a wall can be seen just below the surface of the gardens, indicating that there was indeed another wall. One of the original gate pillars still stands in front of No. 32 Alexandra Road, next to the garage. These walls marked the boundaries of the kitchen garden or another part of the Cambridge estate, and may date from the period of owner-ship under Henry Bevan, rather than earlier.

Bevan died at Cambridge House on 11 September 1860 at the age of eighty-four, leaving an estate in the region of £400,000, held in trust for his two daughters. Under the terms of his will, Cambridge House and its contents were left to his eldest daughter, Lady Caroline Mary Chichester. In 1844, Caroline had married Lord John Ludford Chichester (1811–1873), sixth son of the Marquess of Donegal and MP for Belfast between 1845 and 1852. Caroline's younger sister, Louisa Harriet Dean Paul, inherited Bevan's town house in Hanover Square.

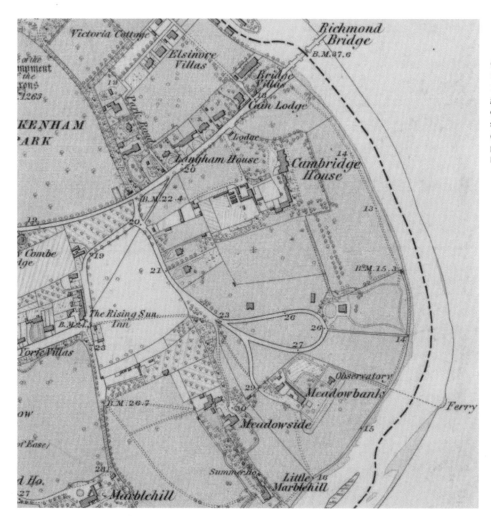

Ordnance Survey map of 1869 (surveyed 1864–1865) showing the kitchen garden, greenhouses and orangery to the west and south of Cambridge House (Reproduced with the permission of the National Library of Scotland)

The will was lengthy but clear, and guarded Mr Bevan's fortune closely within the family. In the event of the death of either daughter, her share of the estate was to pass to the survivor, and after the death of both to Mr Bevan's nephew, Charles James Bevan. Other than a bequest of £300 to each of his two executors, there were no legacies to any further members of the family or servants. Lord and Lady Chichester took possession of Cambridge House in the following year. They had no children, Lady Chichester having married late in life, and lived in grand style, maintaining an indoor staff of twelve and an outdoor staff of seven.

Lady Chichester was to remain in situ until her death in 1883, witnessing much of the later nineteenth-century development in the western part of the original Cambridge Park estate, centred around today's Cambridge Park road.

CHAPTER 11
BISHOP'S OBSERVATORY AND HAVERSHAM GRANGE

The new owner of Meadowbank in 1861 was Mr George Bishop, whose father had recently died. The late George Bishop was a noted astronomer, regarded as being in the front rank of amateurs and was at one time President of the Royal Astronomical Society. Several major discoveries had been made from his observatory in Regents Park, but recently there had been 'frequent interruption from the lights and smoke of London'.

In 1863, the younger George Bishop removed his father's original dome, instruments and valuable library and set up an observatory in the grounds of his new house at Twickenham, which promised 'a site possessing a very open view of the southern heavens'.

The observatory built by George Bishop at the north end of the Meadowbank site (By kind permission of *Illustrated London News*/ Mary Evans Picture Library)

The position of the new observatory had been carefully determined astronomically and geodetically with the assistance of the Director-General of the Ordnance Survey, Sir Henry James (1803–1877). The equatorial room containing the telescope measured 15 feet in diameter with a dome rising to 18 feet 6 inches, and the observing chair gained for its maker the medal of the Society of Arts. A transit room, library, sleeping apartment and storage room completed the observatory, all under the supervision of the late Mr Bishop's assistant, Mr John Russell Hind (1823–1895), who had moved his family to Twickenham.

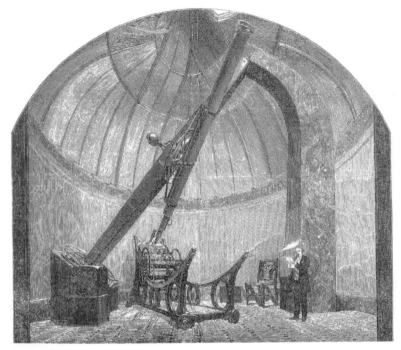

Left: Interior of the observatory (*Illustrated London News*, 9 October 1869), with the observing chair (By kind permission of *Illustrated London News*/ Mary Evans Picture Library)

Below: The observatory by the river, with Richmond Hill in the background, right, with the Star and Garter Hotel in a previous incarnation, c.1868, from George Bishop's personal photo album (Howard Webb Collection)

Having sold Meadowbank to the delighted Mr Bishop, John Parson built for himself a house on a large plot by the river adjoining the grounds of Cambridge House, which he named Haversham Grange.

At the time of the sale, Mr Parson and Mr Bishop also exchanged restrictive covenants establishing a building line across the properties, from the southern-most boundary of Meadowbank to the northern boundary of Haversham Grange, beyond which no building was to be allowed, other than 'a boathouse, arbour or summerhouse not exceeding 12 ft in height'.

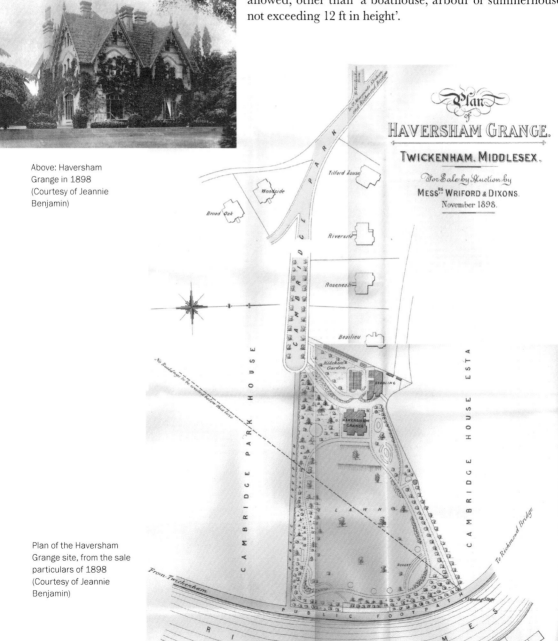

Above: Haversham Grange in 1898 (Courtesy of Jeannie Benjamin)

Plan of the Haversham Grange site, from the sale particulars of 1898 (Courtesy of Jeannie Benjamin)

Jeannie Benjamin, who spent some time in Haversham Grange in the 1940s when it was converted into council flats, wrote about the house in 2020: 'It was fascinating to read all the details about the house sale [in the 1898 auction sale particulars]. Those rooms must have been truly magnificent. What we called the woods were then known as 'well-timbered pleasure grounds', what we called the orchard was known as the 'kitchen garden' and what we knew as the bombed house was the 'stabling'. It certainly was a paradise for me, my sister and the other children in the flats.' (See also Chapter 22.)

In the 1860s, the existing carriage driveway from the north entrance at Richmond Road was proving inadequate, and on 20 May 1862, John Parson and Major Jelf Sharp entered into an agreement to create a new road serving their respective properties, as shown on the Ordnance Survey map of 1869. A private footpath led from this road down to the river.

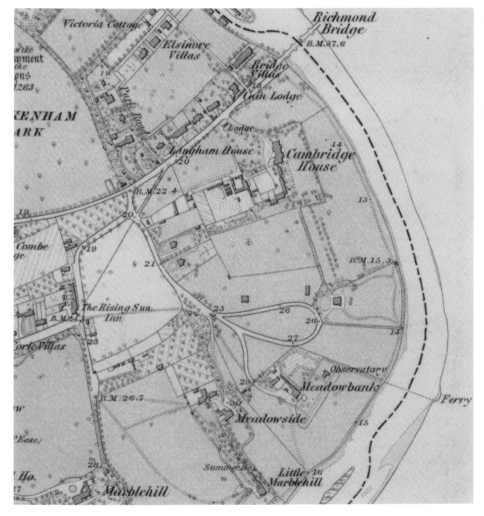

Ordnance Survey map of 1869 (surveyed 1864–1865) showing Parson's and Sharp's new road to serve their respective properties. Haversham Grange itself is not named.
A private footpath led from this road to the riverside.
(Reproduced with the permission of the National Library of Scotland)

Meadowbank and the Observatory seen over the river from Richmond (Howard Webb Collection)

This new road was to be laid and maintained at their joint cost, and until such time as the road was dedicated to public use, 'gates of neat and ornamental design' were to be erected at their mutual expense at the north entrance to this road. As long as the gates remained, John Parson agreed to 'duly provide a fit person to reside in the existing lodge to have charge of such gates and to open and close them for the use of the tenants or occupiers of the houses on the respective properties of the parties ...'

Whether these gates were ever installed is doubtful, as within a year of that agreement, on 7 April 1863, John Parson sold off the balance of land amounting to 15 acres 35 roods, 'together with all and singular road ways ... trees woods etc' to Mr Jeremiah Little, a Kensington builder, for the sum of £8,000, securing for himself a profit of £4,000 in just over two years.

Meadowside and the land belonging, including the Ten Acre Field, remained the property of Major Jelf Sharp. Employing a team of thirty-five men, Jeremiah Little now proceeded over the next five years to build the estate of grand Victorian villas which he named Cambridge Park (see Chapter 13).

George Bishop sold Meadowbank by auction in 1877 for £14,000 and retired to the South of France. The telescope and other apparatus from his observatory he presented to the Capodimonte Astronomical Observatory at Naples, Italy, where they remain to this day.

The house changed hands several times more. Lily Langtry, the actor, and mistress of King Edward VII, first trod the boards in an amateur production in Twickenham town hall and is reputed to have rented it at one time.

The observatory building was finally demolished in the early 1960s by its then corporate owners. The extensive wooded grounds have remained, but a new house was built on the Haversham Grange site in 1980, designed by architects Rosenberg & Gentle, accessible via what is now Haversham Close.

"MEADOWBANK,"
TWICKENHAM MEADOWS,
MIDDLESEX.

PARTICULARS, PLAN, VIEW AND CONDITIONS OF SALE
OF AN EXCEEDINGLY CHOICE

Freehold Residential Property
SITUATE

ON THE BANKS OF THE THAMES,

Near Richmond Bridge and the Orleans Club, and within a short distance of Three Railway Stations, and Richmond Park, and amidst some of the most

Beautiful Scenery of the Valley of the Thames,

Opposite the celebrated Star and Garter Hotel, and the Duke of Buccleuch's Residence at Richmond, Petersham Meadows, &c.

THE MANSION
Contains ample Accommodation for a Family of Distinction, with

EXTENSIVE STABLING AND PREMISES,
GAS AND WATER ARE LAID ON THROUGHOUT,

THE GROUNDS OF 9¼ ACRES
ARE NICELY DISPOSED IN

Lawn with Flower Beds, & studded with fine old Timber,

BROAD GRAVEL WALKS AND TERRACE, LARGE CROQUET AND TENNIS LAWNS

Summer House, Shrubbery, Rustic Bridge,

AND LARGE MEADOW SKIRTING THE RIVER THAMES,

VINERY, CUCUMBER HOUSE, BOAT HOUSE & other Outbuildings,

THERE IS ALSO A SUBSTANTIALLY ERECTED

Observatory, until recently used for Scientific and Astronomical purposes,

WITH TWO ROOMS, STORE CLOSET, LAVATORY, W.C., &c.

The whole forming one of the most complete Riverside abodes that could possibly be met with so near London, within easy driving distance of the Clubs, Kensington Gardens, Prince's, &c., and in such a favourite and healthy Neighbourhood!

Which will be Sold by Auction,
BY

MR. CHANCELLOR

AT THE AUCTION MART, TOKENHOUSE YARD, CITY,

On TUESDAY, THE 5TH DAY OF JUNE, 1877,

At 1 for 2 o'Clock.

The Property may be viewed by orders to be obtained of the Auctioneer. Particulars with Plan and Conditions of Sale obtained at the Auction Mart, Tokenhouse Yard; of FRED. CHANCELLOR, Esq., Architect and Surveyor, 8, Finsbury Circus, E.C.; of Messrs. BRACKNBURY & THOMPSON, Solicitors, 17 and 18, King's Road, Bedford Row, W.C.; and of Mr. A. CHANCELLOR, Auctioneer, Land and Estate Agent and Valuer,

1, KING STREET, RICHMOND, SURREY.

Printed by Thomas Scott, Warwick Court, Holborn.

Above: Sale notice of
Meadowbank, 1877
(Richmond upon Thames
Local Studies Library
and Archive)

Left: Haversham Grange,
c.1929, from the sale notice
(Richmond upon Thames
Local Studies Library
and Archive)

CHAPTER 12

THE EXILES CLUB AND BEYOND

In December 1919, Meadow Bank was purchased by the Eastern Telegraph Company (later Cable and Wireless Ltd) for use as a club for their overseas employees. The official opening of the Exiles Club, as it was to be known, took place in June 1920, attended by more than one thousand five hundred people. There were complaints of overcrowding and criticism of the catering arrangements, resulting in a shortage of tea and sandwiches.

The *Evening News* of 18 October 1922 reported that membership of the Exiles Club totalled some three thousand, and it owned 20 acres in Orleans Park with an up-to-date pavilion, two rugby, two football and two cricket teams, a ladies hockey team, swimming teams and more:

> 'A more ideal spot for exiles home on leave from such remote spots as the Cocos Islands, Perim, Labuan Island (off Borneo), and other lonely stations belonging to the company in the Near and Far East could not be imagined … The title Exiles Club originated many years ago among a very small party of men engaged on the lonely cable station 10 miles from Lands End.'

The original Meadowbank, together with Mr Bishop's Observatory, was demolished between 1961 and 1962 and a new clubhouse opened on the site in 1963.

The Exiles Club, c.1930s, making good use of the Archdeacon Cambridge's final home (Postcard image provided by Kenneth Lea)

Nationalised by the British government in 1947, Cable and Wireless continued as a global operation, but in Britain itself functioned as part of the Post Office, within the former state monopoly on telecoms. It was eventually privatised in the 1980s.

4. EXILES CLUB, *from Lawn.*

Postcard dealer Alan Winter, who grew up locally, recalls: 'The Exiles Club sports ground and clubhouse were on the site of the current Orleans Park School. There were two entrances: the main one being behind Orleans Lodge on the Richmond Road and the second opposite the Marble Hill Park Gate in Orleans Road. The house opposite the gate is called Park Cottage and for many years was the home of Mr Ryde who was the Exiles Club groundsman. We used to go to birthday parties for his son Johnny Ryde there. It was a strange cottage in that it has a very large room which looks as if it must have been a hall of some sort at some point.'

The Exiles Club lounge, 1938, from the company staff magazine, *The Zodiac* (Richmond upon Thames Local Studies Library and Archive)

The Exiles Club from the riverside, 1934, also featured in *The Zodiac* (Richmond upon Thames Local Studies Library and Archive)

In the early 1990s, there was for a short period a private members' sports and leisure club in the grounds called the Meadowbank Club, but this has since been turned into a residence.

Today's Lynde House Care Home, to the north, and the sports and leisure club to the south were built in 1995. Keith Whitworth Architects then converted the sports club into a private residence in 2002–2003: Keith Whitworth had worked for MacCormac Jamieson Prichard architects (MJP), in 1995, when the two buildings were first constructed. MJP designed the sports club, but not Lynde House, although they were responsible for the masterplanning of the overall site.

Obtaining approval from the now disbanded Royal Fine Art Commission, the government's independent adviser on matters affecting public amenity and aesthetics, was described by Keith Whitworth as 'a battle, as the site partly sits on Metropolitan Open (protected) Land. In fact we had to move the building further away from the Thames until we finally got approval. The buildings' impact as seen from Richmond Hill was also a very important consideration.' The site was eventually recognised with a Civic Trust Award.

The original design as a social club for Cable and Wireless was adapted into a private single residence. The two-storey-high living room space now serves as the formal dining and sitting room, with large glazed elevations that overlook the 12 acres of the mature landscaped gardens running down to the Thames. The ground-floor bar and kitchen facilities were removed and converted into a kitchen, breakfast room and library or retreat. The first floor was converted from conference and meeting rooms into bedrooms and overhanging offices. One storey is underground, previously the gym and changing facilities, and now bedrooms, bathrooms and a games area.

Twentieth-century corporate ownership and later redevelopment may have increased the density of buildings on the north-west side of the site, but the river approach to the south-east has remained as open ground, despite the suburban development closer to Richmond Bridge. The legacy of the eighteenth- and early nineteenth-century grand houses and gardens persists here to this day, although the story of later Victorian builders was far from complete.

Meadowbank
as converted in
2002-2003 by Keith
Whitworth Architects
(Photos and drawing
by Keith Whitworth
Architects)

KEY

▽ ▽ ▽ METROPOLITAN OPEN LAND LINE

Above: The architect's plan shows the Lynde House Care Home to the north of the converted Meadowbank.

Meadowside, now rebuilt as Art Deco flats with extensive grounds, sits to the left of the Meadowbank house (in black) in this plan. Meadow Lodge (house) lies to the west of Meadowbank – above with this orientation. (Plans by Keith Whitworth Architects)

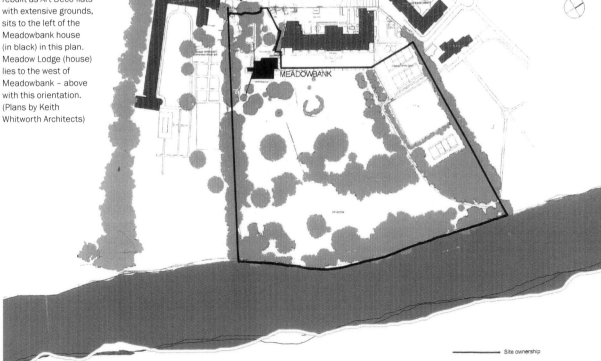

Site ownership

CHAPTER 13
THE 19TH-CENTURY DEVELOPERS

Jeremiah Little was a prosperous and respected builder from Kensington, where he employed some sixty hands. His sons Henry, Alfred James and William worked with him in the business, which between 1848 and 1873 was responsible for the building of more than one hundred and fifty houses in the Camden Hill area.

The expanding railway system was focusing attention on the outer areas of London, and the discontinuation of tolls on Richmond Bridge in 1859 now made the riverside on the Middlesex bank an attractive proposition for development. Cambridge Park was Mr Little's first and, many would say, highly successful venture into the suburbs.

After 1860, John Parson's loop-shaped road was straightened to form the road that today leads to the footpath to the river, and building began immediately. On 1 September 1863, the first villa was leased to Mr William Eales while still under construction, and over the next four years, sixteen further substantial detached villas were built on the fifteen-acre site purchased from Mr Parson. In laying out the new estate, Mr Little was careful to retain many of the fine trees that had existed in Archdeacon Cambridge's grounds.

With the partially developed new estate proving successful, the Littles began negotiations in 1864 to 1865 with Major Jelf Sharp for the purchase of the Ten Acre Field. The Major was at that time living in Kincarrathie, Scotland, while Meadowside Cottage was leased to the Dowager Countess of Harberton.

Shortage of funds still appeared to feature in the Major's life. In April 1858, he had mortgaged Meadowside Cottage to Lord Petrie for £3,000 and in 1861 had taken out a further charge, again with Lord Petrie, for £2,500. By 1864, he was being pressed for repayment, and after transferring both these mortgages to the Revd William Jelf and Henry Willis, a banker, the Major promised to repay Lord Petrie, explaining that 'he had had considerable expense in making roads … and had now contracted to sell certain portions of the estate'.

Meadowside Cottage was enfranchised from the Duke of Northumberland at Sion on 27 November 1862, and the sale of the Ten Acre Field as freehold land to Jeremiah and Henry Little was completed on 28 July 1866. A small portion of the kitchen garden was retained for the use of Meadowside Cottage (compare Ordnance Survey maps of 1869 and 1894).

An ancient right of way had long been established over the Ten Acre Field, posing some difficulty with the layout of this new section of the Cambridge Park estate. Through many generations, the people of Twickenham had taken a shortcut across the fields, from the Rising Sun pub to a point in the Richmond Road opposite Park Road, over time forming a public footpath. To keep this right of way open, the Littles utilised the path as a boundary between two rows of houses. On the west side, facing the Richmond Road, they built five houses known as Beaufort Villas, with rear gardens backing on to the path (these became Nos. 310–318 Richmond Road).

On the east side, seven pairs of five-storey semi-detached houses were built with rear gardens leading on to the other side of the footpath, which was subsequently paved and is known today as St Stephen's Passage (formerly St Stephen's Lane). These houses were numbered 1–14 Cambridge Park Gardens.

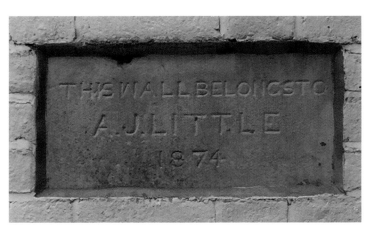

(Photo by
Jonathan Crofts)

Following the line of the old carriageway from the entrance opposite the Rising Sun, six more detached villas were built, with one separate coach house and stables for Mr Alfred Little's own use, and these completed the triangle surrounding what is now the site of the Cambridge Park Bowls Club. The coach house is now a private residence, hidden behind a 1930s house. A wall at the rear where it adjoins the former kitchen garden of Meadowside still bears a plaque reading 'This Wall Belongs To A.J. Little 1874'.

Former resident Margaret Wilson recalls: 'Our back wall was the park wall of Marble Hill Park. In my day we often had people walking up the long drive, thinking that it was an entrance to the park. My grandfather and great uncle bought the property between them in 1919, the idea being to use the land as a market garden, to grow vegetables for my grandparent's greengrocer's shop in Richmond Road. This plan obviously did not work out long term, since they sold off the land for number 18 [the 1930s house] to be built. My mother, Beth White, lived in the house her whole life and my brother and I sold the property in 2007 following her death. Originally the building consisted of stables, the coach house and a tack room on the ground floor, with a flat for the coachman on the first floor.'

Between 1863 and 1868, the Littles built a total of thirty-seven houses on the Cambridge Park estate and five in the Richmond Road. The larger, detached villas with sweeping carriage driveways were set in plots varying from one-third to a whole acre, and prices ranged from £1,000 to £2,000. Some were rented out at £50 per year. The largest plot covered 4 acres, on which Henry Little built Cambridge Park House for his own use (on the site today of Cambridge Park Court and The Old Garden). The smallest villas contained eleven rooms, excluding kitchens and sculleries, and the largest fifteen rooms. Mains water provided cold water to sculleries and WCs, but bathrooms were still a luxury of the future. Lighting was by means of oil lamps and candles.

The old lodge by the Rising Sun was demolished to make an entrance to coach houses and stabling behind the houses backing on to Marble Hill Park, known as Beaufort Mews. Cambridge Park Mews, consisting of sixteen coach houses and stabling with living accommodation above, was built to the rear of the lodge at the north entrance to the estate (see the Ordnance Survey map 1894 on next page).

One of the villas has not survived, however. Margaret Wilson saw the flats at Parkview Court under construction in the mid-1970s: 'I remember Parkview Court being built while I spent time in the garden revising for my university 'finals' exams! Unfortunately it replaced a lovely old Victorian villa similar to that at number 17. The driveway up to Parkview Court used to be part of our garden ...'

Meadowbank and Meadowside Cottage, together with Haversham Grange, Cambridge Park House and several of the larger villas, had coach houses and stables within their own grounds.

The community came from the prosperous middle classes. Residents included bankers, stockbrokers, solicitors, barristers, a magistrate, physicians, retired military gentlemen and one or two merchants; many were of 'independent means'. The Census for England and Wales, 1881, provides us with an insight into the standard of living of this affluent Victorian neighbourhood. Thirty-five households were returned by the enumerator. Of these, twenty-one families produced a total of seventy-two children. One hundred and twenty-two servants were employed, and every household had a cook, supported by parlour, house and kitchen maids. There were eight children's nurses. Governesses, of whom there were three, had the social misfortune to stand somewhere between the family and domestic staff. The Dowager Countess of Harberton and her daughter, the Hon. Esther Pomeroy, maintained an establishment at Meadowside Cottage employing six indoor staff, including a butler and a personal lady's maid. The coachman lived above the stables.

Conservatories were a popular addition to many houses. Several gardens were laid with tennis courts and croquet lawns, which quickly formed part of the social scene, and a plan of 1898 shows the present site of the Cambridge Park Bowls Club as 'A.J. Little – Tennis Lawns and Gardens'. However, petty crime followed the whiff of privilege, and the *Richmond & Twickenham Times* of 5 June 1875 carried an alarming report that 'several garden robberies have taken place in the neighbourhood of Cambridge Park during the last few nights. Consequently the residents will do well to take care of their outdoor treasures'.

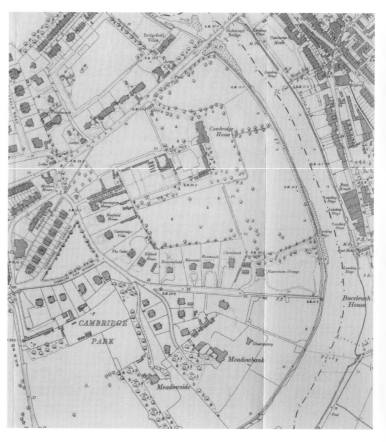

Ordnance Survey map of 1894 (revised 1893–1894) showing the north Lodge and Cambridge Park Mews, and Beaufort Mews north of Marble Hill Park (Reproduced with the permission of the National Library of Scotland)

In 1878, a decision by the Local Board to replace the house names in Cambridge Park with numbers met with strong opposition, and a memorial signed by the local residents requesting the Board 'to proceed no further with their proposal' was presented. Mr Alfred Little said that it 'was certainly objectionable to the inhabitants and was quite unnecessary as the houses were all named and there was no difficulty in finding them'. Col. Elliott of Belcamp pointed out that residents would be put 'to a considerable inconvenience in having to change their notepaper, cards, plates, dies etc. It would also destroy the rural character of the neighbourhood and do it considerable harm'. The scheme was dropped, and numbers were not introduced until 1912–1913.

In Cambridge Park, progress continued and in November 1887 all houses were connected to the main sewerage system laid by the Local Board. Gas was also introduced in that decade, but it was not until 1902 that electricity was connected, supplied by the Twickenham and Teddington Electric Supply Company.

A major change took place at Cambridge Park House, purchased by Sir John Whittaker Ellis, Bart., MP, JP, from Henry Little in July 1896 for £4,750. Sir John (1829–1912; Lord Mayor of London 1881–1882, and Charter Mayor of Richmond 1890–1891) was at that time living in Buccleuch House, Petersham Road, on the opposite bank of the river. The grounds surrounding Buccleuch House were small, the gardens at the rear having been sold to Richmond vestry by the previous owner to form part of the Terrace Gardens. The meadowland stretching from the formal gardens fronting Cambridge Park House to the river were now transformed into pleasure grounds for Sir John, his family and guests, who were rowed across the river to sample their delights (see also Chapter 24).

Conservatory at Cambridge Park House, from the auction catalogue of Buccleuch House (on the Richmond side of the river) (Richmond upon Thames Local Studies Library and Archive)

Described at the time as having been 'laid out at very great cost being one of the best specimens of modern landscape gardening in the neighbourhood and forming a most delightful source of amusement and recreation', the grounds had spacious lawns, and walks terminating in vistas containing statuary. An Italian garden with an ornamental fountain near the centre, tennis and croquet lawns, and a bowling green, completed the landscaping.

Sir John's most extravagant gesture was the demolition of the existing villa, scarcely thirty years old, to be replaced by a very large conservatory built on the same foundations. Forming part of this conservatory block was a 'Garden House comprising capital reception rooms, with ornamental fireplace and statuary marble chimney piece; large Cloakrooms and expensively fitted up Lavatories having Hot and Cold water supplies etc'.

Behind the conservatory was a house for the head gardener, also vineries and glasshouses; and the laundry was 'fitted in a perfect manner for the most economic working, comprising a Wash house with five troughs with hot and cold water, an ironing room, and drying yard'.

Other later Victorian notables living in Cambridge Park included Edward Stanley Gibbons of stamp-collecting fame at Cambridge Villa; Ivy Compton Burnett, the author, as a child at Chesilbank (later Beaulieu); and Sir Henry Evan Murchison James, top-ranking civil servant in India at Glenshee.

Above: The gardener's house and conservatory were demolished between 1934 and 1936, and the site then reallocated to Cambridge Park Court, a block of 36 flats, and a house known as The Old Garden (not the same building that bears this name today).
(Photo by Jonathan Crofts)

Glenshee from the carriage approach (above, left) and the grounds (left), from the sale notice (Richmond upon Thames Local Studies Library and Archive)

Field-Marshal Lord Birdwood (1865–1951) led the Anzac forces at Gallipoli in WWI, and lived at Dalkeith House in Cambridge Park. William Riddell Birdwood was born in India, and commissioned in the 4th battalion, Royal Scots Fusiliers, in 1883; he then joined the 12th Lancers in India in 1885. In 1894, Birdwood married Janetta Hope Gonville (1879–1947), daughter of Sir Benjamin Parnell Bromhead, 4th Bt., with whom he had two daughters and a son.

Birdwood's army career took him to South Africa, becoming deputy-assistant adjutant-general to Lord Kitchener in 1900, and his military secretary in India in 1905. His long professional relationship with Kitchener (later the British Secretary of State for War) had a strong influence on his career. Promoted to colonel in 1905, he rose to the rank of major-general by 1911. He received a Distinguished Service Order (DSO), was mentioned in dispatches, and made a Companion of the Indian Empire (CIE).

He stayed in India until 1914, as secretary to the government in the army department, and was then, as lieutenant-general, appointed corps commander to the Australian and New Zealand (Anzac) forces sent to Egypt. His involvement with the infamous Gallipoli campaign culminated in his successful leadership of the evacuation in 1915–1916.

He had become formal administrative commander to the Australian minister of defence in 1915, and led the Australian Corps to France in 1916. Knighted that year, he was made a general in 1917, and appointed to command the Fifth Army in May 1918. Created a baronet in 1919, his final promotion was to Commander-in-Chief, India, and Field Marshal in 1925.

Described as having 'unconcealed eagerness for personal recognition' in the *Oxford Dictionary of National Biography*, he failed in his desire to become Governor-General of Australia, but retired from the army to become Master of Peterhouse, Cambridge, from 1930–1938. In 1941, he published *Khaki and Gown: An Autobiography* (Ward, Lock & Co).

In 1935, he was appointed Captain of Deal Castle and in 1938 was created Baron Birdwood of Anzac and Totnes. After a life filled with honours, he is buried in Twickenham Cemetery.

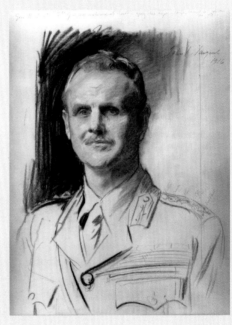

William Riddell Birdwood, first Baron Birdwood (1865–1951) by John Singer Sargent, 1916 (© National Portrait Gallery, London)

Until the late nineteenth century, East Twickenham remained extremely rural. One interviewee told of a childhood in Cambridge Park in the 1870s when the gardens at the rear of her parents' house, Beaconsfield, still led on to the fields attached to Cambridge House.

Another account from the 1880s described the walk from the family home at Yelverton Lodge, opposite Marble Hill Park, to Richmond, 'passing The Rising Sun and through a passage called St Stephen's Passage between the Church and the backs of the houses in Cambridge Park, and it passed on into a small footpath bounded on the right by the palings of Cambridge Park and on the left by the low wooden palings of a kitchen garden which belonged to Cambridge House, and which had on the west side a bank crowned with very fine globe artichokes, handsome in flower. The road continued to Richmond Bridge with the Park palings on the right-hand side all the way. The road used to be considered the most beautiful road out of London. On each side were trees and at the foot of the Bridge was a group of may trees [hawthorns], which were a sight when in full flower.'

In the 1870s, Richmond Road was purely residential, with six large houses and gardens on the north side, and a small lodge on the corner of Park Road. Of those today, only Ryde House and Willoughby House still remain.

At Cambridge House, one member of the Bevan family still lingered on. Following the death of her husband Lord John Chichester in 1873, Lady Caroline Chichester remained in the vast house for a further ten years until her own death in 1883. She died intestate, leaving an estate valued in excess of £150,000. Both her sister Louisa Paul and cousin Charles James Bevan were already dead. Letters of Administration were granted to Edward John Dean Paul (later Sir Edward, the 4th Baronet) of Hyde Park Corner, her nephew and only next of kin, the only surviving son of her sister Louisa.

Sir Edward and Lady Eliza Monckton Paul, a granddaughter of the Earl of Dalhousie, retained their house at Hyde Park Corner and divided their time between town and Twickenham. A mere three years after moving to Cambridge House, Lady Paul died and Sir Edward placed a handsome stained glass window in the sanctuary of St Stephen's Church in her memory.

Shortly after taking possession of Cambridge House, Sir Edward fell foul of the Local Board when, without consultation, he erected railings on both sides of the old towpath at the end of his grounds, in order to prevent pedestrians from crossing his lawns. The Highway Authority took Counsel's Opinion and were advised that the path was an ancient highway and that pedestrians 'might deviate to a point where dry land existed when tides and floods rendered the path impassable'.

In 1887, an amicable agreement was reached between the Local Board and Sir Edward, resulting in the Board making a footpath 12 feet wide, and Sir Edward erecting iron railings on his side of the footpath. The Board then agreed to maintain this footpath and the embankment in good repair. This was the beginning of the Warren Footpath which today runs from Richmond Bridge to Orleans Road.

Since at least 1866, gates or turnstiles had been erected across the old towpath at the boundaries of each adjoining property: Haversham Grange, Cambridge Park House, Meadowbank, Meadowside Cottage and Marble Hill. In 1889, the Local Board requested the removal of these obstacles, and five years later stated their intention of repairing the footpath, apportioning the cost between the owners of these properties (excluding Marble Hill) to a sum of £85.1s.11d. Strong objections were raised and it was considered that the 'proposed works were unreasonable and the estimated expenses excessive'. After a hearing before the Justices in July 1896, the cost was reduced to £22.6s.9d. That same year, the Local Board assumed responsibility for ongoing repairs to the footpath.

Sir Edward's death in 1895 resulted in the eventual sale of Cambridge House. The parkland around it was ripe for suburban development and in another ten years it would be home to hundreds of families, part of a growing Christian population that rapidly filled the large capacity of the newly built church.

ERNIE LOTINGA.

Ernie Lotinga, born 1875, was a star of the cinema and music hall in the 1920s and '30s. He and his second wife, Kathleen, also an actor (1893–1952), lived in Beaconsfield, 36 Cambridge Park, until his death in 1951. His son Paul continued to live there until the early 2000s.

From a wealthy Danish–Jewish family, Ernie used to sneak in to watch music hall shows as a boy. He started his career singing before becoming an established music hall performer during the 1890s. He was well known as a pantomime dame. He toured Asia, Australia and the US with his first wife, Hetty King, and eventually became an impresario, writing, directing and producing.

In WWI, Ernie and Hetty performed for the troops in France and Belgium. At the outbreak of WWII, he once again entertained troops as part of ENSA (Entertainments National Service Association) and broadcast radio shows to boost morale. His most famous character, 'Jimmy Josser', was disparaging of authority and featured in a series of bawdy, knock-about comedy films.

Ernie is featured in the sculpted frieze on the Odeon cinema in Shaftesbury Avenue. It pictures him in a role in *Khaki*, a 1924 farce set in wartime. He was the favourite comedian of poet T S Eliot, whose masterpiece *The Waste Land*, written in the years just after WWI, reflects the devastation of that war. Eliot wrote about him to author Virginia Woolf (another resident of Cambridge Park, in the nursing home at Burley, No. 15): 'Have just been to see Ernie Lotinga in his new play at the Islington Empire. Magnificent. He is the greatest living British histrionic artist, in the purest tradition of British obscenity.'

Dr George Simmers, an expert on World War I fiction, blogged in 2008:
'T.S. Eliot was a big fan ... and references to Lotinga as an exemplary kind of music-hall artist crop up in Eliot's critical writings over a long period. [Lotinga] made several films, starting in 1929. That date should give the clue that he was essentially a verbal comedian, and so was sought after for the movies when sound came in... He's a high-energy performer. Eliot talks of his anarchic character and ... his bawdy [chat]... This, I think, is what Eliot liked in Lotinga's ... performance – a defiance of dull naturalistic logic, and a determination to live every moment to the full.'

Left: One of the many characters played by Ernie Lotinga (Photos by permission of Dr George Simmers, Great War Fiction blog: www.greatwarfiction.wordpress.com)

The Odeon Covent Garden was built in 1931 as the Saville Theatre and became a cinema in 1970. Its Art Deco façade has a stone frieze by sculptor Gilbert Bayes depicting 'Drama through the Ages'.

On one corner is a figure in soldier's uniform. Although art critics originally saw it as 'a sombre moment in an otherwise exuberant piece', the figure is now believed to represent Ernie Lotinga in *Khaki*, a farce about military life.

The success of the show may have been due to the reaction of the Lord Chamberlain in his role as theatre censor, who wrote 'the play is a farrago of idiocy, vulgarity and sham sentiment'.

Lotinga's own response was: 'My burlesque is pure harmless fun, and as I am solely a burlesque comedian, the only way I can obtain my laughs is by doing or saying something absurd. I find it most interesting to see the weight of the Establishment come crushing down on a farcical and rather silly play like *Khaki*.'

St. Margaret's, Richmond.

CHAPTER 14

CHURCH AND CHAPEL

After a long stint of service in the navy, Captain John Gray in 1718 sank his earnings into the purchase of land close to the river and along the western border of Marble Hill estate to build homes for 'respectable citizens of Twickenham'. Montpelier Row and the adjoining Sion Row, as he named them, were to have their own chapel and school to serve the householders and their families and staff. Gray obtained approval from the Bishop of London to build the chapel and appoint his own chaplain. An engraved communion plate, now held in St Stephen's Church, commemorates the opening of the chapel in 1720.

A century after this, the rail service operated by the London and South Western railway was extended in 1848 to Twickenham, and in 1873 residents petitioned for a local station at St Margarets. One of the key petitioners was Henry Little, the property developer, who owned Cambridge Park House and had begun to develop the new residential area of Cambridge Park for the bankers, lawyers and business owners who sought a tranquil life on the outskirts of London (see Chapter 21).

The Rising Sun pub with the tram service running past St Stephen's Church, c.1905 (Howard Webb Collection)

With the coming of the railway, the population quickly expanded and Montpelier Chapel, designed to accommodate some two hundred and fifty souls, was now too small. The Little family donated land bounded by the Richmond Road and the ancient right of way now known as St Stephen's Passage. The triangular plot explains why the church is not built facing east as would be more customary for an ecclesiastical building, but in fact looks north. In the eighteenth century, the site had been a brickyard.

St Stephen's Passage, by the lychgate to the church, 2020 (Photo by Jonathan Crofts)

St Stephen's Passage was originally an ancient right of way over the Ten Acre Field. It was clearly shown on the Ordnance Survey map of 1869, leading to Richmond Road.

Most of the passage survives as a right of way, but a short stretch behind the shops and businesses on Richmond Road can only be seen if visiting the dentist Toothbeary, at the corner of the set-back shops on the south side of the road.

The cost of the new church was valued at £7,000, and Henry and Alfred Little, who were committee members, stipulated that building was not to commence until at least £3,000 had been raised. The appeal was well supported and by 1 August 1873 was oversubscribed. Henry Little donated £100, and £50 was received from Charles James Bevan, heir to Cambridge House. Architects were invited to tender designs for a church to seat one thousand people.

Lockwood and Mawson, best known for their work on the model community of Saltaire in Yorkshire, received the commission and drew up sketches for a church built from Kentish rag and Bath stone. The foundation stone of the Church of St Stephen was laid on 28 September 1874 by the Duchess of Teck, mother-in-law of the future George V; her country residence was at White Lodge in Richmond Park, now home of the Royal Ballet School. In October of the following year, an Order in Council created the new parish of East Twickenham.

By 1 December 1875, the foundations for the whole church were complete, but only the nave was ready for consecration by Bishop Claughton, suffragan to the Bishop of London. The first vicar was Reverend Francis Moran, who had served as minister at Montpelier Chapel, and he presented a brass plaque listing the Chapel incumbents to the church. The Reverend lived at No. 21 Cambridge Park, which served as the vicarage until 2010. Henry Little was appointed as the first people's churchwarden.

The south transept and the organ chamber were consecrated in 1885 by the Bishop of Bedford, William Walsham How, then suffragan to the Bishop of London, and later Bishop of Wakefield. He was known as the writer of rousing hymns such as 'For all the saints who from their labours rest' (1864). The north transept was dedicated in 1893 by Frederick Temple, the Bishop of London himself. It was not until 1907 that the consecration of the bell tower by the first Bishop of Kensington, Frederick Ridgeway, marked the completion of the external structure. During the period from 1905 to 1911, a chancel screen, designed by George Halford Fellowes Prynne, was erected as part of an improvement of the chancel area.

St Stephen's Church, c.1910 (Postcard image provided by Kenneth Lea)

A prayer book recording marriages between 1729 and 1752, together with some silver, were brought over from the Montpelier Chapel. The church finally became operational in 1876, and the now redundant chapel was sold and used as a public hall and then a laundry, before eventually collapsing in 1941. A modern house was built on the site. The private home in nearby Orleans Road, mistakenly called 'The Old Chapel', was in fact the original Montpelier School building.

In 1896, a chapel was erected by St Stephen's on the northern edge of the parish to serve the residents of the workers' cottages in the area now bounded by Winchester Road and the Chertsey Road. This building is now used by St Stephen's School, which was built at around the same time.

Henry Little (left, with full beard), Chairman of Twickenham Urban District Council, at the opening of York Street, 1 March 1899 (Richmond upon Thames Local Studies Library and Archive)

Henry Little remained a churchwarden for many years and it is believed that the church was consecrated in the name of St Stephen in honour of the date of his wife's birthday. The carved stone fruit and flowers on the capitals of the pillars were modelled on the flowers and fruit flourishing in Henry Little's garden.

With the building of St Stephen's Church, Jeremiah and Henry Little's development of Cambridge Park was complete, and their design was to remain intact for nearly a century. Jeremiah Little himself did not live to see St Stephen's Church complete in its entirety but died in 1873, leaving a string of properties in Cambridge Park to his sons, Henry and Alfred. The rate book for 1875 shows Henry and Alfred Little as owning between them twenty houses, sixteen stables and a workshop. Henry Little lived on at Cambridge Park House until his new development at The Barons (on part of the old Twickenham Park estate in St Margarets), was ready in the 1870s, when he went to live at Baronsholt, No. 14. Alfred Little lived in Cambridge Park until his death in 1897, aged fifty-five.

Henry Little became deeply involved in local affairs and between 1869 and 1911 was a member of the Twickenham Local Board (converted to an Urban District Council in 1894). From 1899 to 1900 he was chairman of the Council and in the same year was appointed to represent the east electoral division of Twickenham on the Middlesex County Council, a post he held until his retirement in 1911. He died in 1914.

The Centenary Room was created from the West (South) door entry area between 1975 and 1976 to mark the anniversary of the opening of the church. The

internal space within the body of the church was dedicated by the Archdeacon of Middlesex, the Revd John Perry, in October 1976, and is used for weekday activities, with catering facilities for cooking main meals.

St Stephen's Church in the early 20th century (Howard Webb Collection)

The need for more space to develop work with children and young people led to a prolonged fund-raising campaign, which produced The Crossway next to the church. This was officially opened in 1999 by the Bishop of Kensington, the Rt Revd M J Colclough. The same year saw the setting up of the Crossway Pregnancy Crisis Centre in an adjacent building, also for community and church use, to support those facing the trauma of an unplanned pregnancy or pregnancy loss. Out of this grew a charity in 2005, seeking to support women and their partners in the boroughs of Richmond, Hounslow and Kingston. Its ethos is that 'no woman should have to go through the experience of considering having an abortion, or dealing with a miscarriage or past abortion, without being supported'.

In the 1990s, a generous anonymous donor also enabled comprehensive modernisation in the church building itself. The floor of the chancel was extended into the nave, and the choirstalls and stone screen were removed, with a baptistry installed beneath the staging. In the nave itself, the old pews were replaced by chairs, and a new wooden floor and modern lighting and heating installed.

An extension to the church called The Spring was built alongside St Stephen's Passage and opened in 2011 by the Bishop of Kensington, Paul Williams. Stones from the arched windows of Montpelier Chapel were used to create a bench outside the new extension. In 2013, the Ark Room (the old choir vestry) was transformed into a secluded area for individual contemplation called the Prayer Chapel.

The interior of the church has some fine examples of Victorian stained glass, mostly from the hand of Alfred Octavius Hemming (1843–1907), a descendant of two of the ministers of the old Montpelier Chapel. The confirmation candidates between 1881 and 1886 presented the five lancet windows to either side of the West door, while the three clerestory windows depicting St Patrick, St Alban and St Aidan were given by the confirmation candidates of 1902 and 1903.

The church's proud evangelical tradition is commemorated by stone carvings below the clerestory windows showing the heads of the leading Protestant reformers in England. Cranmer, Latimer, Ridley, Bradford and Hooper were all despatched at the stake; only Wycliffe escaped, although his bones were ceremonially disinterred and burned nearly one hundred years after his death. Unfortunately, the stone heads cannot be linked to their individual names. Two of the heads are now hidden by the ceiling of the Centenary Room.

The foundation stone laid by the Duchess of Teck lies beneath the middle lancet window when approaching the West door from outside. The inscription has sadly long since eroded away. The brass plaque by the kitchen door, given by the first vicar, lists the ministers of Montpelier Chapel. St Stephen's also rejoices in one of the best preserved 'Father Willis' pipe organs in London, first dedicated in 1889, just as the parish served by the church was really starting to change.

The exterior of St Stephen's Church, later in the 20th century (Photos © St Stephen's Church)

The interior photos of the church probably date from soon after its completion in around 1880 and certainly before 1907, when the tower was added: the pulpit shows no clouding of the marble that can be seen today. A stone rood screen, not in line with the evangelical tradition of the church, was put in place by a High Church vicar c.1935 to screen off the chancel; the congregation voted to remove it in around 1980 in order to make better use of the chancel space for worship.
(Photos © St Stephen's Church)

CHAPTER 15
EARLY 20TH-CENTURY EXPANSION

When Sir Edward John Dean Paul died in 1895, his estate passed to his son, Aubrey Edward Henry Dean Paul, 5th Baronet, but in his will, he expressed the wish that Cambridge House should be sold. It was placed on the market in 1896, giving rise to considerable local fears and misgivings. *The Builder* magazine for May of that year said:

> 'The projected sale of Cambridge House and grounds at Twickenham for building purposes seems to presage the demolition of a house which, in the latter half of last century was the resort of the many celebrated friends of Richard Owen Cambridge.'

The *Richmond & Twickenham Times* carried an article by 'Professor Democritus Dart' who wrote:

> 'I hear various rumours as to the future of that portion of the riverside at Richmond Bridge surrounding Cambridge House. I will challenge almost any part of the Thames to show a fairer scene than that which this beautiful park presents, viewed either from the Bridge or from the opposite bank. I fear it is doomed. The rumour goes that the meadow is to be raised to the level of the present path and that building operations will then set in severely. Heigh ho! More bricks and mortar! I am glad I am not going to live another fifty years.'

Cambridge House and the surrounding 30 acres of parkland was sold in March 1897 to Henry Cresswell Foulkes, a builder from Hornsey in North London, fulfilling the worst fears of local residents. Mr Foulkes took up residence in Cambridge House, retaining for his own use the grounds immediately surrounding the house, and the lawns stretching down to the river, together with the entrance drive and lodge at the main gates in Richmond Road.

The rumours regarding development were confirmed when building operations began in the parkland. The walled kitchen garden with its forcing houses was demolished, greenhouses and vineries were razed to the ground, and lawns and paddocks disappeared under the foundations of the new estate. Joining Henry Cresswell Foulkes in this development was another family member, Morley Punshon Foulkes, also a builder, from Leyton in East London.

By the end of the century, hundreds of houses had sprung up along four new roads: Cresswell and Morley (perpetuating the names of Messrs. Foulkes), and Alexandra and Denton. Henry Cresswell Foulkes planned his estate on a grid system and in contrast to the large detached houses built by Henry Little in adjoining Cambridge Park, built smaller two-storey terraced and semi-detached houses.

Along the south side of Richmond Road, he erected a parade of shops with living accommodation above from the corner of Cresswell Road to Morley Road, and by the turn of the century, this line of emporia, named Cambridge Parade, extended all the way to the corner of Alexandra Road. The old sub-Post Office in East Twickenham, which now serves as a convenience store, was known as the Cambridge Parade Post Office.

On the north side of Richmond Road, Mr Foulkes then built two more stretches of shops with flats above. The block from the corner of Park Road to the former National Westminster Bank (corner of Rosslyn Road) was for a time known as Richmond Parade, and a smaller block nearer the bridge as Richmond Bridge Mansions Parade.

The corner of Morley Road and Richmond Road, with J. Clarke and Sons Dairies on the right (Howard Webb Collection)

The new 'shopping centre' of East Twickenham provided a variety of services.

Clarke & Sons dairy was on the corner of Morley Road and Richmond Road, and included a sub-post office. (Later the premises became Hornby & Clarke, before being taken over by Express Dairies until about 1970.) Clarke & Sons advertised their speciality of 'Nursery Milk from our own Jersey cows kept at the Home Farm, East Twickenham'. Josiah Clarke had run a dairy business on Hill Rise, Richmond, since 1881 and in 1908 he moved his family (he fathered eighteen children) to Park Lodge, Park Road, and installed his cows on the Home Farm meadows opposite (now the site of Beresford Avenue, north of Richmond Road).

Alongside the staple tradesmen of butchers, grocers and fruiterers, such as Forrest's Stores at No. 28, shops of a more exotic nature also catered to the residents: 'Madame Louise, Milliner', 'Taizan & Co., Oriental Bazaar' and 'Madame Suzanne, Antiques'.

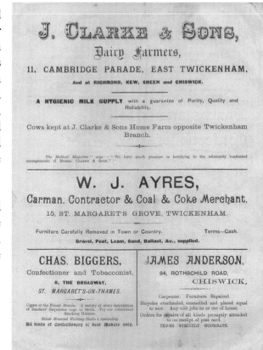

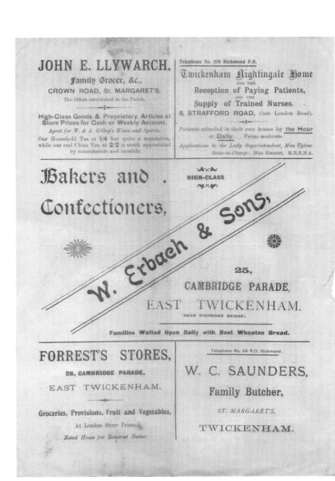

JOHN E. LLYWARCH,
Family Grocer, &c.,
CROWN ROAD, St. MARGARET'S.
The Oldest established in the Parish.

High-Class Goods & Proprietary Articles at
Store Prices for Cash or Weekly Account.

Agent for W. & A. Gilbey's Wines and Spirits.

Our Household Tea at 1/4 has quite a reputation,
while our real China Tea at 2/2 is much appreciated
by connoisseurs and invalids.

Telephone No. 379 Richmond P.O.

Twickenham Nightingale Home
FOR THE
Reception of Paying Patients,
AND THE
Supply of Trained Nurses.
6, STRAFFORD ROAD, (late London Road).

Patients attended in their own homes by the Hour
or Daily. Terms moderate.

Applications to the Lady Superintendent, Miss Upton.
Sister-in-Charge: Miss Knight, M.R.B.N.A.

Bakers and
Confectioners,

HIGH-CLASS

W. Erbach & Sons,

25,
CAMBRIDGE PARADE,
EAST TWICKENHAM.
(NEAR RICHMOND BRIDGE)

Families Waited Upon Daily with Best Wheaten Bread.

FORREST'S STORES,
26, CAMBRIDGE PARADE,
EAST TWICKENHAM.

Groceries, Provisions, Fruit and Vegetables,
At London Store Prices.
Noted House for Somerset Butter.

Telephone No. 54 P.O. Richmond.

W. C. SAUNDERS,
Family Butcher,
ST. MARGARETS,
TWICKENHAM.

There was also a branch of the London & County Bank, a house furnishers, a jeweller and a bicycle shop.

The chemist at No. 18 Cambridge Parade exists today with its original sign of Charles Harry.

The name of Cambridge Parade was dropped when the Richmond Road was renumbered between 1909 and 1910.

Erbach & Sons, the baker at No. 25, had its own bakehouse at the rear, and survived into the 1960s.

Clarke's milk float (Richmond upon Thames Local Studies Library and Archive)

The *Richmond & Twickenham Times* of 21 September 1899 carried the following report:

'Building operations in Alexandra Road are now being completed and nearly all the houses are occupied. There are thirty houses, letting at £36 per annum. In Morley Road there are 14 semidetached houses each of the rental value of £42. The houses in Cresswell Road are of a better class. There are only eight semidetached and one detached house. They are of the bay and Venetian bay style, prettily ornamented with white stone. These will let at over £50. On the main road there are ten shops between Cresswell and Morley Roads and from Morley Road, already six and the idea is to carry them all the way along. The corner shops are letting at £110 per annum, and the others at £100 per annum, one of which has just been taken by a draper.

The work is not entirely new to Mr. Foulkes as there are evidences of his work in this direction in North London. It was a huge undertaking to buy such a property as Cambridge House and open it up in a neighbourhood as it is. There are naturally prejudices ... but it is as we have previously remarked, a natural consequence of our nearness to the Metropolis, and the rush there is for living in the suburbs.

Before the work is finished, we believe some hundreds of houses will be erected. This is a vast increase ... and was not expected a few years back.'

Cambridge Parade, with horse-drawn and motorised vehicles in the early 20th century. Note the lack of shops on one side, later replaced by Richmond Parade. (Postcard provided by Ashley Hinton)

Twickenham.—Richmond Road.

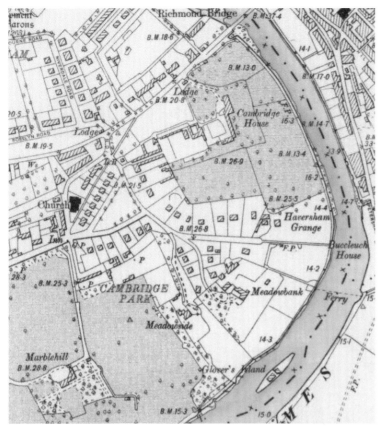

Henry Foulkes completed his development over the first ten years or so of the twentieth century. He encountered similar difficulty with St Stephen's Lane (or Passage) as had Mr Little some forty years earlier, but in October 1902 succeeded in gaining permission for the right-of-way to be 'turned, diverted and stopped-up', enabling the completion of Cambridge Parade to the corner of Alexandra Road (see Ordnance Survey maps 1894 and 1939).

By 1907, the large iron gates to the entrance of Cambridge House had been removed and the lodge demolished, to be replaced by Richmond Terrace, a block of eleven shops running from the corner of Cresswell Road to the newly laid Cambridge Road. Building also started on Clevedon Road at this time.

Top: Ordnance Survey map of 1894–1896 (revised 1893–1894), prior to the development by Henry and Morley Foulkes: the north-east section of St Stephen's Passage is still in place (Reproduced with the permission of the National Library of Scotland)

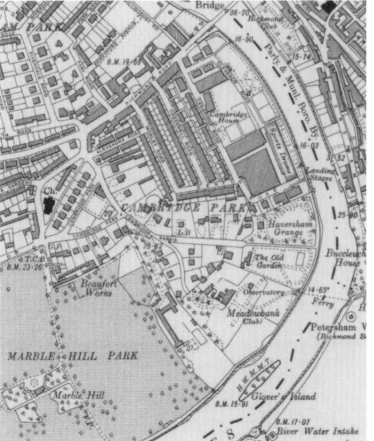

Left: Ordnance Survey map of 1939 (revised 1934–1935), following the suburban development. Cambridge House is still shown, although it had in fact been demolished in 1937. The north-east section of St Stephen's Passage has now been subsumed into the shops. (Reproduced with the permission of the National Library of Scotland)

This Indenture *made the Fourteenth day of July One thousand nine*
hundred Between HENRY CRESSWELL FOULKES *of Cambridge House Twickenham*
in the County of Middlesex Gentleman (hereinafter called " the Lessor") of the one part
and MORLEY PUNSHON FOULKES *of 2 Calderon Terrace Leyton High Road*
in the County of Essex Builder (hereinafter called "the Lessee") of the other part
Witnesseth *that in consideration of the expenses incurred by the Lessee in and about the*
erection of the messuage and premises hereinafter mentioned and of the rent and covenants
hereinafter reserved and contained and on the part of the Lessee to be paid and performed
He the Lessor Doth hereby demise unto the Lessee All *that piece of land situate at*
Twickenham in the County of Middlesex abutting towards the North-East on Morley Road
Twickenham Together with the messuage or dwelling-house outbuildings and premises erected
thereon and Numbered 40 in Morley Road aforesaid And which said premises hereby demised are
delineated on the Plan drawn on the first page of these presents and are thereon coloured Red
And the appurtenances Except nevertheless and reserving full right of passage and
running of water and soil from all neighbouring lands and houses belonging in possession or
reversion to the Lessor through all drains channels and sewers in or under the said piece of land
hereby demised To hold *the said premises unto the Lessee for the term of Ninety-nine years from the*
Twenty-fifth day of December One thousand eight hundred and ninety-seven Yielding and Paying
therefor during the said term the
yearly rent of Eight Pounds Ten
Shillings *by equal quarterly pay-*
ments on each of the usual
quarter-days without deduction
(except for property tax on the rent
hereby reserved) the first quarterly
payment to be made on the
Twenty-ninth day of September
One thousand nine hundred And
the Lessee doth hereby covenant with
the Lessor That the Lessee will
at all times during the said term
pay the said yearly rent of Eight
pounds ten shillings on the days and
in manner aforesaid And will
also pay and discharge all present
and future taxes rates charges and
outgoings of every description for
the time being payable in respect of
the premises and including therein
the sewers rate paving or roadway
rate and all rates and charges for
drainage or private improvements or
public works and all others which
but for this covenant would be
payable by the Reversioner (the
property tax on the said rent only

Indenture for 40 Morley Road from 1900, showing the plot and the names of the two builders/developers, Henry Cresswell Foulkes and Morley Punshon Foulkes These houses were at this stage all held in leasehold.
(Photo by Jonathan Crofts)

Right, top: Cambridge House, East Twickenham, seen from Cambridge Road in 1910. This entrance lay at the rear of the building. Note the building beyond. This was the bus garage straddling Cambridge and Clevedon Roads, since replaced by modern town houses.

Right: Cambridge House seen from across the river in Richmond, 1904. The grand frontage of the house faced the river.
(Both photos courtesy of Richmond upon Thames Local Studies Library and Archive)

Sale notice from 1928 for 25 Morley Road, at this time still 'held on lease for a term of 99 years from December 25th, 1897'
(Richmond upon Thames Local Studies Library and Archive)

LOT 2

The conveniently situated Re-decorated

Modern Residence

of pre-war construction.

25, Morley Rd., Twickenham

Situate in a pleasant residential neighbourhood, just off the main 'bus route, 3 minutes from Richmond Bridge and convenient for either St. Margarets or Richmond Stations.

The Residence which is of attractive elevation is brick built and slated, and is approached from the road from a tiled forecourt protected by a dwarf wall and iron palisading.

The Accommodation provides on the

GROUND FLOOR—Dining Room measuring 18ft (into bay) by 11ft 6in fitted with tiled stove, Drawing Room 17ft 6in by 12ft 6in with French casement to Garden and tiled stove, Kitchen fitted with kitchener, dresser and store cupboard, Scullery with glazed sink (h. and c.) and Copper, Larder, and outside W.C. Roomy Tiled Hall with useful cupboard under stairs.

FIRST FLOOR—Front Bedroom 17ft 6in (into bay) by 15ft 6in with tiled stove and wardrobe cupboard, Linen Cupboard on Landing, Two other Bedrooms measuring 13ft by 11ft 6in and 10ft 6in by 9ft each fitted with stove, Bathroom fitted bath and lavatory basin (h. and c.), Separate W.C. A Tradesmen's Entrance is provided with direct access to Kitchen.

At the rear is a PRETTY GARDEN.
The House is wired for Electric Light. Gas laid on.

Held on Lease for a term of 99 years from December 25th, 1897, subject to a Ground Rent of £8 10s. 6d. per annum.

Vacant Possession on Completion of Purchase.

Cambridge House from
Cambridge Road, c.1900
(Richmond upon Thames
Local Studies Library
and Archive)

Interior of the gracious
entrance hall and staircase
with fireplace and pilasters
supporting a frieze,
Cambridge House, c.1910.
All of the architectural
features were demolished
along with the house.
(Richmond upon Thames
Local Studies Library
and Archive)

Richmond Mansions block of mansion flats in 2020 (Photo by Jonathan Crofts)

Building land was becoming scarce and prices were escalating, making smart mansion flats a popular solution. These were springing up all around London.

Henry Foulkes built seven such blocks. Clevedon Mansions, on the corner of Richmond and Cambridge Roads, had two shops on the ground floor, one a tobacconist, the other tea rooms.

After this came Heatherdene on Cambridge Road; then Balmoral, Riverview, Cambridge Court and North Court on Clevedon Road; and, at the river end of Denton Road, Richmond Mansions. A similar ornamental design can be seen over each of their entrance porches.

Henry Cresswell Foulkes' ambitious scheme came to a halt when he was declared bankrupt in July 1908. During his eleven years in East Twickenham he had built more than one hundred and sixty houses, fifty-four shops with associated living accommodation, and seven blocks of luxury apartments.

Cambridge House was sold, and for some years was the home of the Middlesex County Club. In 1915, it reopened as The Cambridge House Residential Hotel, advertised as:

This Noble Mansion with spacious grounds formerly the home of the Earl of Chichester, containing a magnificent entrance hall, suites of reception rooms, ballroom etc is NOW with his wife and servants room £3.3s. Central heating. Gas fires and slot meters in bedrooms. A tennis club in connection with above; ten courts, four winter (en tout cas) and six grass.

Under the proprietorship of Mr. & Mrs. Wm. Wilson. Telephone Richmond 1294.

In 1921, however, Henry Cresswell Foulkes made a comeback to the area. His subsequent company, Property Agents and Owners Ltd., purchased Poulett Lodge in

Twickenham, where he lived in its eighteen bedrooms with his wife and servants until his death in March 1925, aged seventy-eight. All he left was a small legacy to a secretary and effects worth £187.

In Cambridge Park, the triangle in the centre known as 'Mr. A.J. Little's Tennis Lawns and Gardens' had become disused and overgrown with weeds, and in 1920 was acquired by the Twickenham Bowling Club (who had previously played on a green attached to The Rising Sun pub nearby). The 'Cambridge Park Bowling and Sports Club' was founded by William Poupart and eight fellow local businessmen. A bowling green and five grass tennis courts were laid, and the club opened with its first match on 23 May 1921.

A pavilion was added in 1922 and expanded in 1927 – the perfect setting for the club to host a Middlesex County Bowling Association match against Australia. Estimates for new outdoor and indoor greens were sought in 1945. In 1956, the pavilion was enlarged again, with two indoor rinks constructed. In 1967, a new clubhouse with four indoor rinks and other modern facilities replaced the hard tennis courts. The old pavilion was then leased out.

Entrance to Cambridge Park Bowls (Bowling) Club in 2020 (Photo by Jonathan Crofts)

Although the postcard caption indicates an aerial view of Richmond, the bulk of the view is of East Twickenham, dated 1920. It shows the bus garage, factories and a derelict Cambridge House in Cambridge Road. (Postcard image provided by Kenneth Lea)

AEROFILMS SERIES   AERIAL VIEW OF RICHMOND TOWN   No. 1693

Today, the club plays friendly matches against other local clubs and belongs to a number of different competitive leagues. Affiliated to the Middlesex County Bowling Association, its members compete in county and national competitions. The club has a licensed bar, kitchen, dining area, lounge and changing rooms.

Alfred Little's coach house remains, tucked behind a house built in the orchard in the 1930s.

The former coach house of Alfred Little, pictured in 2006
(Photo by Margaret Wilson)

Along the river a new promenade was raised well above the level of high tides, as flooding had become a serious problem. This promenade 'was overhung by splendid old trees and flowering bushes under which are a sufficiency of strong and comfortable seats' and the Warren Footpath was opened in June 1923 by the Duke of York (later King George VI).

Cambridge Gardens officially opened on 6 July 1929, with the Mayor and chairman of the Pleasure Grounds Committee (of Twickenham) in attendance. Tea was served on the balcony of the Ice Rink, there was an enjoyable putting match between officers of Richmond and Twickenham Borough Councils, and a tennis competition between representatives of local tennis clubs.

Meadowside Cottage (see Chapter 9) came under threat in 1909 after the death of the then owner, the Revd G L Rudd. His trustees wished to sell the property and prepared plans for houses to be built on the upper part and business premises on the lower, asking a price of £7,000 for the six-and-a-half-acre site. This would have seriously affected the view from Richmond Hill, protected earlier with the purchase of Marble Hill by the London County Council and others in 1902 (see Chapter 16), and all efforts were now made to place restrictive covenants on Meadowside not to construct buildings below a specified line.

The entrance to Meadowside in 2020
(Photo by Jonathan Crofts)

A purchaser was found who was willing to give these covenants but requested in compensation a payment of £1,000. The money was raised with the London County Council contributing £500, the Twickenham Council £200, and Richmond Council the balance of £300, and Meadowside Cottage remained a private property. When the house was finally demolished in 1934 and replaced by a block of flats in the Art Deco style, the gardens were preserved, of which several features remain to this day.

In the same decade, six houses were built on the side lawns of Burley, No. 15 Cambridge Park. For many years Burley was a nursing home (described as 'a polite madhouse for female lunatics') and Virginia Woolf was a patient there on three occasions, in 1910, 1912 and 1913.

These large Victorian villas, with the inconvenience of kitchens and sculleries in the basement and the growing unwillingness of women to enter domestic service, were becoming both difficult and expensive to maintain, and during the 1930s many were subdivided into flats.

Cambridge House, now completely surrounded by buildings, was demolished in 1937. Outstanding architectural features were destroyed along with the building, including carved pine and oak panelling and mahogany doors of the seventeenth century, together with several splendid fireplaces and a particularly handsome staircase. The *Richmond & Twickenham Times* commented:

> 'The deterioration of this part of Twickenham lies partly at the door of the estate developer who built the flats already standing at each end of the land, and partly the Council, which permitted the retention and development of the Pelabon Works [see Chapter 17] … when the War was over.'

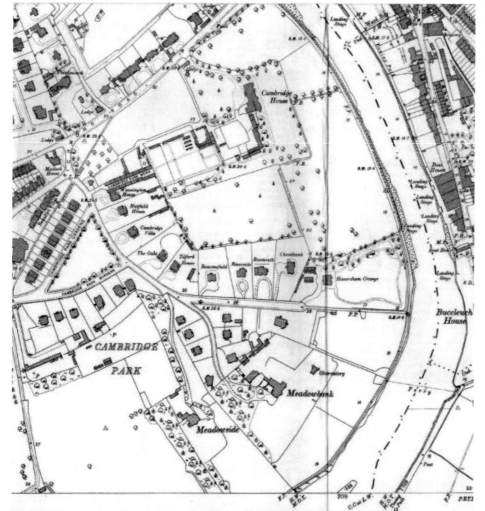

Ordnance Survey map of 1894 showing the names of the larger Cambridge Park villas (Map image provided by Kenneth Lea)

Henry Cresswell Foulkes' original layout of roads and houses remained almost unchanged, other than the development of Cambridge Road and the addition of Nos. 1–23 Cresswell Road some time after 1910. Between 1910–1914, the land on the west side of Cambridge Road was sold, and terraces of houses constructed along its length. By that stage Foulkes' surburban houses and mansion flats were complete, and the view from Richmond Hill over Richmond Bridge and East Twickenham riverside would be changed for ever.

Mansion flats on Cambridge and Clevedon Roads in the 1930s (Howard Webb Collection)

CHAPTER 16
SAVING THE VIEW FROM RICHMOND HILL

The view from Richmond Hill over Petersham Meadows, Richmond and the East Twickenham riverside had long been memorialised by famous painters such as Reynolds, Gainsborough and Turner (see Chapter 1). The two former artists had houses on Richmond Hill, and Turner at Sandycombe Lodge on the other side of the water.

Turner's painting *Richmond Hill, on the Prince Regent's Birthday* looks across Richmond Hill towards Twickenham, and was exhibited in 1819. The image can be seen on the Tate website (www.tate.org.uk). According to the Tate gallery label from 2019, '*The Examiner* newspaper described it at the time as "a pictorial display of the magnificence of England". The painting was Turner's attempt to attract the patronage of the Prince Regent, the future King George IV. The prince was an increasingly unpopular figure, due to his extravagant lifestyle and his poor treatment of his wife, Caroline. Turner failed to get royal support, and his picture was seen as a bit pretentious. Looked at in the context of the political upheaval of 1819, Turner's idyllic landscape could be accused of being strikingly out of touch.'

A view of the River Thames from Richmond Hill, c.1752, by Francesco Zuccarelli (1702–1788) (© Sotheby's 2021)

Zuccarelli's perspective, similar to one exhibited by Turner in 1819, may feature some measure of artistic licence – it includes more grand residences than the view by Augustin Heckel (see Chapter 1).

The hillside grounds of Buccleuch House and Lansdowne House on Richmond riverside were initially consolidated by the Duke of Buccleuch in the 1860s and on his death were bought by the Richmond vestry to help preserve the renowned view from Terrace Walk, opened to the public as the Terrace Gardens in 1887. Glover's Island (Petersham Ait), just below, was saved from the dire fate of advertising Pear's Soap and presented to Richmond in 1900 by the wealthy businessman and philanthropist, Sir Max Waechter (1837–1924), who could appreciate the river scene from his home in Terrace House, above Terrace Field.

A new and significant threat to the view came in 1899–1900 from William Cunard, of the shipping dynasty, whose agents were negotiating with Twickenham to construct housing estates at Marble Hill as well as Lebanon Park.

However, in 1900, Marble Hill was purchased for the public, funded by nineteen private benefactors and five local authorities, including Twickenham and Richmond. Another authority, London County Council, began advertising Marble Hill Park as an asset for the enjoyment of people from across the capital. Much of the opposite riverside also became public property through the Richmond, Petersham and Ham Open Spaces Act of 1902.

From 1899 onwards, however, the once bucolic outlook over Twickenham Meadows was increasingly consumed by the myriad roofs of Henry Foulkes' extensive development, as well as new streets south and east of Richmond Road with their own grids of housing. Today, only pockets of green survive from the old Cambridge Park estate on the Meadowside, Meadowbank and Haversham Grange sites, beside the still lush lawns of Marble Hill Park.

Richmond Bridge seen from East Twickenham, c.1900
(Howard Webb Collection)

The campaign to save the vista over the Thames Vale had been taking place along-side deliberation over the tram routes between Twickenham and Hampton Court (see Chapter 21). On Good Friday 1903, the new Hampton Loop trams towards Twickenham and Richmond Bridge carried some two hundred and fifty thousand passengers, and six hundred and forty-six thousand over the entire Easter holiday. The hallowed view had been preserved in essence, but this moment initiated the most dramatic change in the East Twickenham area, with people able to flock to the area for work or to live in the new houses.

While Cambridge House itself was lost in 1937, with some of its gardens now made public, monitoring of the view continues: the Meadowbank social and sports club was redeveloped at the end of the twentieth century, but negotiations with the then Royal Fine Art Commission resulted in shifting construction further north and away from the river (see Chapter 12).

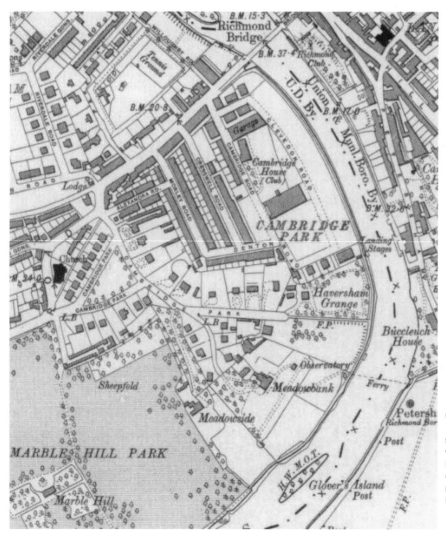

Ordnance Survey map of 1920 (revised 1910–11), showing how the local view had changed from Richmond Hill (Reproduced with the permission of the National Library of Scotland)

In an ever-changing local landscape, the view remains precious and, thanks to artists, campaigners and legislators, will be maintained for future generations to enjoy. A few years after the 1902 Act, however, World War I brought a major munitions works to the East Twickenham riverside.

Richmond Bridge.

THE APPROACH RICHMOND BRIDGE

CHAPTER 17
'BELGIUM-ON-THAMES'

'Belgium-on-Thames', a pithier version of the historic name for the area's Belgians, was first coined by local resident and historian Dr Helen Baker when she started researching and writing on the subject of Belgian refugees in 2014, a century after the first exiles appeared in East Twickenham. Her work has augmented both local and international understanding of the extent and impact of their migration to south-west London and further afield.

Belgian workers in front of the Pelabon munitions buildings
(Howard Webb Collection)

Dr Baker begins the story: 'Most of the Belgians originally came to East Twickenham and its surrounding areas to work in a vast munitions factory beside the river near Richmond Bridge. Its founder, dynamic Franco-Belgian engineer Charles Pelabon, escaped from Antwerp on the very day it fell to the invading WWI German army, and dedicated himself to the war effort: within only three weeks he was producing shells for the Belgian and Allied armies.

Pelabon had started the Pelabon Works in an empty boathouse in Teddington, which operated alongside the East Twickenham factory for six months. After that, two of the Pelabon directors left to run the Teddington site as a separate engineering works, making war materials for the rest of the duration.'

Shortly after the outbreak of WWI, a letter from Fred W Pearce, the Council Surveyor, drew the attention of members of the Council to a proposal to erect a munitions factory on the land between Cambridge House and Denton Road, fronting Cambridge Road. Charles Pelabon had acquired *'the incompleted building … originally intended for use as a skating rink, and adjoining lands for this purpose'*. It appears that after the failure of an earlier roller-skating rink and its conversion to a bus garage, a further skating rink had been planned for East Twickenham, sited on the south side of Cambridge House (see Chapter 19).

The letter continued:

> '… engineering works in this position would prove of considerable detriment to adjoining property … and having regard to the close proximity of the building to the river and the inclusion of the land in the Town Planning Scheme … it is necessary that immediate action should be taken … as necessary works … have already been commenced.'

A Council resolution was passed that the proposal was undesirable, but it was later agreed to, with the proviso that M. Pelabon should be asked to give up the building for use as a factory within three months of termination of the war. M. Pelabon replied that it would be impossible to remove any buildings within three months and that the minimum period for shutdown would be nearer five years.

Then, on 2 December 1914, the Council received a stern letter from M. Pelabon's solicitors pointing out:

> 'the urgent need of the Allied Governments for immediate delivery of shell cases … and unless facilities can be given by the Council the situation will be calculated to very seriously impede the execution of Government requirements and prejudice the prosecution of the war.'

The Pelabon Works were built by Collinson's Ltd. of Teddington (Howard Webb Collection)

1914-15—THE PELABON WORKS
ARCHITECTE : E. DE NÈVE.
BUILDERS : COLLINSON'S, LTD.

Permission was finally granted and the Pelabon Works shortly thereafter began the manufacture of munitions, mainly shells and gun parts, initially employing several hundred people, largely Belgian refugees. The War Refugees Committee in London deployed a second wave of immigrants in late 1914, mostly affluent Belgians from Antwerp, not all of whom stayed in the area. By autumn 1915, however, the workers included a third wave of some two thousand more exiles, both men and women, recruited from refugee camps in the Netherlands.

Dr Baker continues: 'The refugees largely lived their lives around the Pelabon Works, engaging with its social clubs and welfare services. Not all the Belgians worked in the factory however: desirable Richmond also attracted the wealthier ones, who supported themselves and socialised with their compatriots across London.'

In total, there were six thousand Belgians in the wider community. They lived all over what is now Richmond Borough: in East Twickenham, in St Margarets, where whole streets were often Belgian, and also in central Twickenham, Teddington, Kew, East Sheen and Richmond.

A traction engine with Pelabon workers (Howard Webb Collection)

East Twickenham, central Richmond and Richmond Hill became the heart of a Belgian community which its champion Justin Wallon named 'The Belgian Village on the Thames' in a short book on the subject (*Une Cité Belge sur la Tamise*, 1917). It was known in literary circles that Justin Wallon was a pseudonym, in

English a 'Walloon', meaning a French-speaking Belgian (as opposed to a Flemish-speaking Belgian). Monsieur 'Wallon' was actually Paul Gérardy, a renowned poet and man of letters from Liège in the French-speaking part of Belgium, but at this point a resident of St Margarets.

He was lucky: his forays into journalism quickly won him a position with the Belgian exile press in London. Other professionals, including another poet like himself, were less fortunate with finding white-collar work in England and took manual jobs at Pelabon instead. As M. Wallon put it, this was to occupy their time usefully, avoid relying on charity, and contribute to the Belgian war effort.

Dr Baker notes that Wallon used the French words for 'city', 'town' and 'village' interchangeably, but his wider descriptions make it clear he was thinking in terms of a village: 'There has been some confusion about whether the "Belgian Village" was in Twickenham or Richmond, even on a web-page once posted by the BBC. Wallon himself speaks sometimes of one place, sometimes the other. The (British) residents of East Twickenham themselves have always used the two names loosely. Their lives often connect more to Richmond, just across the river, than to Twickenham, a mile away. Saying that you lived in "Richmond" gave more perceived prestige, certainly in 1915 and still to some extent today; Justin Wallon was not alone in using the terms interchangeably. And so, the numerous mentions of "Richmond" in the text cannot deny the factual evidence that the "Belgian Village" extended on both sides of the river and that its centre-point was East Twickenham.'

The outermost limits of the 'Belgian Village' are difficult to define. As Dr Baker says, the Belgian community took in St Margarets and central Twickenham, and extended into East Sheen and Teddington. Isleworth, the Hamptons, Mortlake and Barnes had Belgian settlements of their own, and Barnes (like Teddington) had a Belgian munitions factory too. All were loosely connected with the Twickenham and Richmond community: local Belgians had involvement with them as well as with Belgian refugees in the greater London region and beyond.

A 'South West London Thames Corridor' running from Chelsea and Fulham out as far as Esher and Thames Ditton, spreading more widely to take in, for instance, Ealing and Wimbledon, has been identified by Dr Christophe Declercq of the University of Leuven in Belgium. Reaching across south-west London, this wider Belgian community lived in parallel with an equally cohesive British community, each going about its own business. For the most part, contact between the two was minimal. Yet Belgians from all these areas and far beyond met together at times, and it is possible that Belgians from some of these other areas even commuted to work at Pelabon.

The Pelabon employees included rehabilitated soldiers and amputees, still viewed as being on active army service, but the Belgian Captain and his detachment of regular soldiers who lodged in a house opposite the site, overseeing quality control in the factory here and elsewhere, were employed directly by the Belgian army.

Wallon had a view of the Pelabon workforce as 'one happy family', although trade unions had to campaign at first for better salaries and there was even, surprisingly perhaps for the period, a call for pay equality across the genders. Belgian pay was soon regulated so that it matched English wages as a minimum. Women were estimated to represent up to a quarter of the workforce, some called 'canary girls' by the English because contact with explosives turned their skin yellow. Foremen and managers were usually men, as were all senior managers.

Many of the Pelabon managers and skilled workers lived in East Twickenham, and there were two rows of Belgian shops here, one by Richmond Bridge and the second further down Richmond Road on the other side. These included a grocer, bookshop, cobbler, jeweller and clock-maker, butcher, tea-house, dressmaker and milliner.

The Pelabon factory's less-skilled workers mostly lived a little further away, many in neighbouring St Margarets, others in central Twickenham and the poorer parts of Richmond. Given the wealthier, self-sufficient Belgians who also lived in Richmond, there were just as many Belgian shops in Richmond itself, but these appear not to have been photographed, perhaps because they occurred one by one rather than in attractive rows.

Perhaps the Belgians' most popular café was a few minutes' walk away at 16 Hill Rise, just over Richmond Bridge, well frequented because it functioned as a brothel alongside serving refreshments. That side of the river also included another café and a Belgian patisserie, a tobacconist and a toy-maker. Furthermore, the Pelabon Company offices were also located in Richmond, in Heron House, of which the seventeenth-century exterior still stands in the Riverside development.

Women, pictured here with male workers and managers, made up some 25% of the Pelabon workforce (Howard Webb Collection)

Right: The Belgian community had their own local shops of all kinds, as well as their own cafés and restaurants, pictured here on Richmond Road (Photos by kind permission of the Royal Museum of the Armed Forces and Military History, Belgium)

Back in East Twickenham, Wallon emphasised the many social activities attached to the Pelabon Works: the social club, orchestra, choir, Walloon and Flemish dramatic clubs, sports club, bowls, dancing, and their pinnacle, the Pelabon Philanthropic Association. Dr Baker has found many other organisations in the wider Belgian community, with a contingent of Belgian Boy Scouts completing the picture. As she says, Belgian life in this attractive and to some extent affluent part of London was diverse and enriching.

Belgian concerts, plays and other forms of entertainment remained largely Belgian and only the Belgian elite had real contact with the English in organised settings. As with the English, the Belgian elite's social activities extended increasingly towards central London, in line with their social status.

A Belgian worker performing acrobatics at the factory (Howard Webb Collection)

The mainly Catholic Belgians did not even meet the English at church, as the local churches held Belgian masses. Belgian education was separate too, either in the special department within Orleans School, Twickenham, or in entirely Belgian-run Richmond schools.

Despite some resentment over Belgians taking over local housing, friendships did occur across the communities, resulting in several marriages and more than one illegitimate child. Most of the couples returned to Belgium after the war, where at least one marriage ended in divorce but the majority continued and produced children.

One example was Edouard (Teddie) Labeye, whose family had fled occupied Belgium early in the war; he was one of five brothers who started work at the factory. In the English community, the death of William Hammerton (of the Twickenham watermen's clan, whose brother Walter ran the ferry by Marble Hill Park) at the Battle of the Somme, left his widow Alice with eleven children and financially hard pressed. As a result, Alice's daughter Nellie Hammerton also began working at Pelabon, where she met Teddie, whom she later married.

A WWI sentry guarding the Pelabon Munitions Works (By kind permission of the Royal Museum of the Armed Forces and Military History, Belgium)

At the end of the war, Nellie and Teddie migrated back to Belgium, where in 1924 they had a son, also called Teddie, who has lived on into his nineties in Brussels.

A century later, in 2014, Dr Baker founded the East Twickenham Centennial Group to celebrate the Twickenham–Richmond Belgian Refugee Community. The Group selected Warren Gardens as the location for a new memorial, just outside the site of the old Belgian factory, where once a sentry guarded the Pelabon Works.

The memorial concept was created by local resident and artist Su Bonfanti in the form of a 'standing stone', with a poetic inscription spiralling around it in a large decorative font, signifying both timelessness and antiquity. It is visible from the Warren Footpath, as well as from the river and Richmond riverside.

The monument was designed by Belgian stone-cutter Kristoffel Boudens and carved by him in Bruges from Belgian bluestone. The inscription was chosen from a poetry workshop at Orleans Primary School, formerly Elementary School, where most Twickenham Belgian children were educated from 1916:

Memories flow through me
like a boat flows down the river

Written by Issy Holton, aged nine, it is carved in the three languages used in East Twickenham in 1914–1918, English, French and Flemish, reminiscent of Wallon's description from WWI (translated by Dr Baker):

'A Belgian who passed Richmond Bridge or walked through the streets around the factory … might well believe he was a victim of hallucination, as he might have the feeling of being suddenly transported to an industrial town in the environs of Liège … Groups stand at street corners and chat gaily. Here and there we hear Flemish or French. But it is Walloon which dominates and one does not hear a word of English.'

The memorial was funded by Richmond Civic Pride and Civic Trust Funds 'with the support of the people of Richmond upon Thames and lovers of Belgium across the world'. The ceremony was supported by the Heritage Lottery Fund, Heathrow Communities Together and East Twickenham Traders Association.

Dr Baker concludes: 'Richmond and Twickenham's Belgian history is unique. Refugees went all over the country, but only Richmond and Twickenham developed a community so large, so compact and so vibrant.'

When the war ended, the Belgians, according to a Borough planning memo, 'melted like snow, leaving so little trace', and by 1945 they were largely forgotten for the next seven decades.

Following seventy years of occupation by engineering and other commercial companies next door to the famous riverside Richmond Ice Rink (see Chapters 18 and 19), the site of Pelabon's factory is now occupied by the Richmond Bridge Estate, a gated expanse of luxury apartments and town houses. Although Pelabon finally left in 1925 to continue his industrial career in France, his name provides some continuity through one of the apartment blocks: Pelabon House.

The memorial was unveiled on 1 April 2017 by the Belgian Ambassador in front of more than 250 people. (Photo by Jonathan Crofts)

CHAPTER 18

THE RICHMOND BRIDGE AND BEAUFORT WORKS

I n the aftermath of the First World War, there were two principal sites for engineering and other works in the Cambridge Park estate area: the Richmond Bridge Works, part of the former Pelabon munitions site, and also Beaufort Works, on the north side of Marble Hill Park (by what is now the car park).

The Pelabon Works did not close as agreed after the Armistice in 1918 (see Chapter 19) but converted its output to general engineering and remained in operation until 1924–1925. From around 1926, the buildings fronting Cambridge Road styled themselves as the Richmond Bridge Works and were occupied by four small firms.

To meet the growing demand for motor cars, Automobiles Berliet had opened splendid showrooms and offices at Sackville Street in central London in 1921, sending a M. Henneguy over from France to run them.

A service and repair depot was set up, initially located at the Richmond Bridge Works in Cambridge Road. They also manufactured a range of vans and lorries.

The company was based here from May 1925 until October 1930, and the site then lay empty until occupied by Wright Brothers (Removals) Ltd. This company was subsequently acquired by Bishop & Sons Depositories Ltd., who were resident until the 1980s.

The parent firm expanded rapidly over the following decades and is still in operation.

Known today as Bishop's Move, it describes itself as the largest family-owned removals and storage company in the UK. Purpose-built removal vans have long since replaced the horse-drawn vehicles they first used, but their distinctive yellow and red livery is still recognisable.

n 1924, part of the old Pelabon factory was turned over to motor manufacturing (Photo of advert from *Commercial Motor* magazine of 11 March 1930, *Grace's Guide to British Industrial History*)

The Richmond Bridge Works had a tradition of hosting metalwork engineering companies. In the 1930s these included Associated Ivorine and Metal Products Ltd., and A1 Nameplate Sign and Novelty Manufacturing Co. Ltd., and in the 1940s Abbot Brown and Sons Ltd, advertising agents, and the Wiles Printing works.

Another longstanding company at the Works was Reliance (Name Plates) Ltd. Originally the Reliance Engraving Co. Ltd. (1904), manufacturers of 'Dials, Scales, Nameplates, Signs, Showcards & Advertising Novelties', it had occupied its Cambridge Road premises since the 1920s.

David King, who lived in Richmond Bridge Mansions, recalls that Ludwig Gmach was one of the managing directors of the Reliance factory. Gmach was born in Munich in 1885 and for a time lodged with David's parents, Gwen Evans-King and Jack King (see Chapter 19). At the start of World War II, Gmach was interned as an enemy alien, but later released because he was Jewish and not seen as a threat. He remained in the UK and died in Hampshire in 1966.

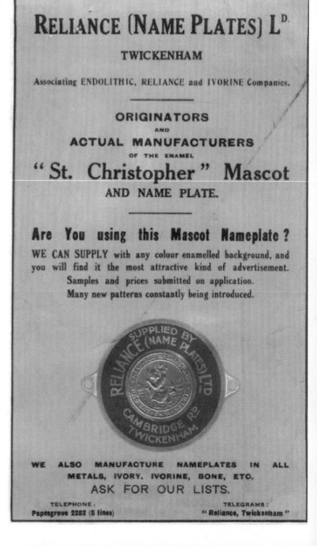

An early advert for Reliance
(Photo by Delphis Antiques)

In the 1920s, Reliance was the third largest producer of celluloid tokens. These were manufactured from prepunched blanks of cellulose acetate strip on standard hand-fed presses.

The company continued to use their original type of press until 1963 when the production of celluloid tokens was finally discontinued.

In 1948, a fire completely destroyed the factory and the company was forced to find new premises. Some unusual tokens were produced prior to the fire, but any reference to them and their production methods were lost in the blaze.

Former employee Nell Best remembers the factory burning down in 1948, and losing her job as a consequence. She recalls leaving work with her friend, and by the time she arrived home in St Margarets, seeing the smoke rising from the factory.

The British Pathé newsreel of the fire, from 3 June that year, reports fifteen fire brigades from all across London responding to the call to save 'tons of highly inflammable cellulose'. Six firemen were injured in the 'three-hour battle', but they prevented the fire spreading to local houses, even though the riverside factory itself was 'a total loss'.

Tony Scott was at the ice rink that day and remembers the 'fire next door in one of the factories, and the ice rink used its fire hoses to cool the rink walls and spray the fire. Mr Arthur Hopkins the Ice Rink Manager directing operations.'

Fires appear to be a theme in the post-war history of this site: in June 1978, a major blaze was occasioned by the summer heatwave.

Patrick Hayworth grew up in neighbouring Denton Road from 1968: 'I skated at the [Richmond ice] rink through most of my teens and was there on the last night for the sit in [see Chapter 19]. We had lived previously in Richmond Mansions and had relatives there until the '90s. I was there when the Paint Store and rear of Bishop's Move warehouse burnt down in the summer of '78. The resulting fire was so intense because of the paint that the brickwork literally crumbled. Beside the paint store was Reliance Name Plates, a factory making badges and name plates for home appliances and the motor industry.'

The fire lasted for so long that local residents Roger Blackwell, his mother and Tony Bagg set up a tea and soup kitchen for the firemen. Anderson Construction was another firm on the site to suffer damage.

By 1983, the name plate company, now known as Reliance Compra, was employing some three hundred people on the site, until compelled by the economic situation to announce redundancies for a third of the workforce. Three years later it took the decision to construct four new buildings in place of the old ones and putting them all up for sale. Reliance also ran a day nursery, which became Twickenham Park Day Nursery when Reliance withdrew from running it in 1982.

Graham Ashurst started work in 1971 in the sales office at Metal Trim Ltd at Richmond Bridge Works, at the end of Denton Road. He remembers colleagues who had been with the company since before WWII. The business had been acquired by Ayrshire Metal Products, probably in the 1930s, and manufactured steel profiles for the building industry, drawer slides and other cold-rolled metal products. In June 1974, due to expansion and issues with loading and unloading the large rolls of steel, the company relocated to Daventry, Northamptonshire. It now operates under the name of Ayrshire Metals.

Arthur Merron in his office at the Richmond Bridge Works (Photo © Ken Merron)

In the late 1940s, Merron Ltd was based at Richmond Bridge Works, making products from laminated or moulded wood.

Arthur Cyril Merron was born in 1902 and started his career producing Art Deco furniture, based in the East End of London and Scotland. He pioneered the process of hot-moulding plywood, which was requisitioned in the Second World War to be used by the De Havilland Aircraft Co. Ltd in Hatfield on the manufacture of the famous Mosquito aircraft.

Merron helped introduce the process for building parts of the aircraft, including the drop fuel tanks, some of which were later used as motorcycle sidecars.

The Merron dinghy, designed by Arthur Cecil Robb, was produced at Richmond Bridge Works: it was the first design to use hot-moulding for a strong, lightweight and stable small boat. Robb, a New Zealander by birth, had originally become yard manager in the 1930s at the boat-building firm of Morris & Lorimer at Sandbank, Argyll, in Scotland.

During WWII, Robb became Lieutenant-Commander in the Royal Navy Volunteer Reserve, and worked with both the Admiralty and Air Ministry. He was later involved with the design of the air-borne lifeboat, with Uffa Fox, an English boat designer. Robb became well known for his cruiser and racer designs throughout the world, especially in the United States, was considered one of the great yacht designers of his generation, and was awarded an MBE.

After the war Merron moved his factory to East Twickenham in 1946, and during his time at the Richmond Bridge Works lived on a boat on the Thames at Eel Pie Island in Twickenham. He cooperated closely with Fairey Marine at Hamble in Hampshire over the years, eventually transferring all his boat-building patents to them in the late 1940s.

The Merron business continued to operate from the Works until his death in 1960, at which point it was sold by the family.

His son Ken Merron remembers the factory well: 'We used to lunch in the Ice Rink – the entrance was opposite the corner entrance to the factory, in Clevedon Road. Merron Ltd. actually occupied the whole of the long frontage facing the rink. The streets were cobbled and used to flood often – sometimes they had to dry out the electric motors as a result. They made boats after the war, including Merron dinghies. After that my father built up a large business manufacturing oak casks for everything from beer barrels to huge ones for shipping palm oil from Africa, that being before the introduction of tank-containers! The unique advantage that he had was that all the compound-curved staves could be manufactured using the same hot moulding technique that had been used for Mosquito parts and the various boats. I remember them off-loading whole tree trunks into the factory.'

Sadly, little is known of Merron's Art Deco furniture today, but the tradition of boat-building continues locally, by Richmond Bridge, on Eel Pie Island and at Isleworth.

The other main engineering site in the area, Beaufort Mews in Cambridge Park, was originally built in the 1860s. In the twentieth century, it became Beaufort Works, the home of various companies.

Beaufort Works were converted to wartime use by Messrs. W.G.C. Hayward & Co., well-known aircraft engineers, according to St Stephen's Church parish magazine of November 1917, 'where amidst surroundings of almost ideal charm and beauty, the firm have constructed what may be fairly described as a model factory for the production of munitions'.

The magazine continued in jingoistic prose typical of the period: 'The history of the concern is at once inspiring and instructive, and illustrates anew those qualities of thoroughness and persistence that have done so much for the industrial supremacy of the British race.'

RICHMOND *from the Air*

A view of 'Richmond from the Air', but which largely shows East Twickenham, c.1935. The early factory units in Cambridge and Denton Roads (just left of centre) remained much the same for several decades. (Postcard image provided by Kenneth Lea)

First established as a private company in 1916, it became a public company in 1920, having had its assets valued at £30,470, excluding 'Goodwill' (*Coventry Evening Telegraph*, 6 March 1920). Before long, however, the *London Gazette* of 11 November 1921 confirmed that the company was being voluntarily wound up 'by reason of its liabilities'.

According to *Grace's Guide to British Industrial History*, the Argson Engineering Co. Ltd. moved here from the West End in 1922. Argson was an acronym made up of the initial letters of the names of the two founding directors, Arnold Ramsden Garnett and Stanley Orton Needham. Following the First World War, their main product was a lightweight 'invalid tricycle', intended for use by ex-combatants who had lost a limb. Sadly, there was a large market for the machines and a company advertisement of 1920 proudly stated that they had sold hundreds to the French government. A R Garnett was himself disabled and had sought to produce a means of transport truly convenient for its owner. The vehicle was powered by the company's own Beaufort 170cc two-stroke engine with, from 1923, the option of an electric motor. In 1924, a novel flat-twin engine was developed from a 175cc engine built to War Office requirements for a generating set. Hugely popular, the tricycle continued in production until around 1930.

For a while Argson also manufactured a lightweight motorcycle, with a two-stroke engine, direct-belt drive and conventional cycle parts, under the Beaufort name. Another version, with a Villiers engine and crankshaft-mounted clutch was also available, but production was sporadic. These machines were typical of the era.

A 1927 report in *The Bystander* read:

> 'In the very early days of the motor car industry Mr. A. R. Garnett, who was a designer and manufacturer of many types of light and heavy automobiles, launched on the market a vehicle known as the National car. Some years afterwards Mr. Garnett was helping a friend to test out another make of vehicle when he met with a very serious accident, which resulted in his being permanently paralysed, and he had to resort to a hand-propelled chair as a means of getting about.
>
> He soon found out that this type of three-wheeled chair was not at all satisfactory, and so he began to design a tricycle which was easy to propel and which would give him exercise, comfort and independence under all varying road conditions. The result is that he is now the manufacturer of the Argson tricycle, which embodies these virtues and is the only machine of its class fitted with a 3-speed gear and differential in the back axle. Its popularity is shown by the fact that, in addition to many hundreds of private users, the Government has taken delivery of over 2,000 of these machines for disabled soldiers. The makers trade under the title of the Argson Engineering Co., Ltd., of Richmond Road, East Twickenham.'

Argson having suffered financial difficulties up to 1930, the vehicle was later made by the Stanley Engineering Co. Ltd of Egham. Stanley Orton Needham had been works director of the Argson Engineering Co. Ltd, with whom he remained for seven years, before founding his own business in 1926, for the manufacture of small petrol sets. He occupied the post of works manager in this firm until his death on 11 September 1933 at the early age of forty-two.

Also at the Beaufort Works, AMD Engineering Co. was founded in 1930 to 'meet the need for the manufacture of high-class precision mechanisms'. Despite being bombed in 1940 (see Chapter 22), the site remained in light industrial use until the 1980s. *International Commerce Magazine* (10 July 1967) reported one hundred and fifty employees, and confirmed its reputation for assembling finished products in addition to making component parts.

An Argson Electric tricycle from 1930
(Photo by Andrew Tweedie)

The founder Mr A McDonald (hence the acronym AMD) was sadly killed in a swimming pool accident in the late 1970s. By the early '80s, the machinery was growing outdated, the management team were no longer in the flush of youth and profit margins were declining. The firm had a wide client base, however, and its assembled products included magnet assemblies for IBM mainframes as well as ticket machines for London Transport. The company clearly still had potential, and in 1981, now with about seventy employees, was acquired by John Watson and other minority shareholders.

In 1982, AMD was joined at the Works by Colne Robotics, a pioneering company founded a year earlier by John Reekie, producing Armdroid robotic arms in kit and assembled form, supported by a camera sensor, Colvis Vision System. Colne employed twelve staff, and in 1983 launched a small robot, the Zeaker Micro-Turtle, designed to be connected to a home computer. Between 1982 and 1983, the company expanded, and almost merged with AMD, which was manufacturing components for it. By 1985, Colne was trading under the name Reekie Robots, selling the 'RUR Hobby Robot', and was proving successful in the US.

AMD was eventually taken over by the Greater London Enterprise Board, but regrettably, a product liability claim in the US led to the demise of both companies, and manufacturing ceased by 1987. The Works buildings were sold on to a property development company, and rebuilt as private flats on the Beaufort Road, overlooking Marble Hill Park, in the 1990s.

AMD Engineering site, Beaufort Works, c.1960 (Richmond upon Thames Local Studies Library and Archive)

Significant factory or production sites no longer exist in the Cambridge Park area, as landowners and developers have exploited the area for housing, although the Richmond Bridge Works endured until the controversial demise of Richmond Ice Rink in the late 1980s.

CHAPTER 19
'THE MOST FAMOUS ICE RINK IN THE WORLD'

The rate books for Twickenham dated 29 October 1910 show that the builder and developer Henry Foulkes owned not only Cambridge House (then occupied by The Middlesex County Club), but also an adjoining property occupied by 'Twickenham Olympia', as well as land in the name of 'Skating Rink Ltd.'.

The latter refers to an enterprise, Richmond and Twickenham Skating Rink Co. Ltd., launched by businessman Charles Bedworth, among others, the purpose of which was to build a roller-skating rink. An advertisement in the *Richmond & Twickenham Times* of 12 June 1909 encouraged investors to buy shares, with the inducement that Mr Bedworth 'believes that the shareholders will receive dividends much in excess of their capital invested within the first year ...'

It was noted that Mr Bedworth was either or both managing director and chairman of four other such rinks, in Harrogate, Oldham, Bolton and Leamington.

Proposed roller-skating rink, 1909 – originally planned for The Broadway in St Margarets (Richmond upon Thames Local Studies Library and Archive)

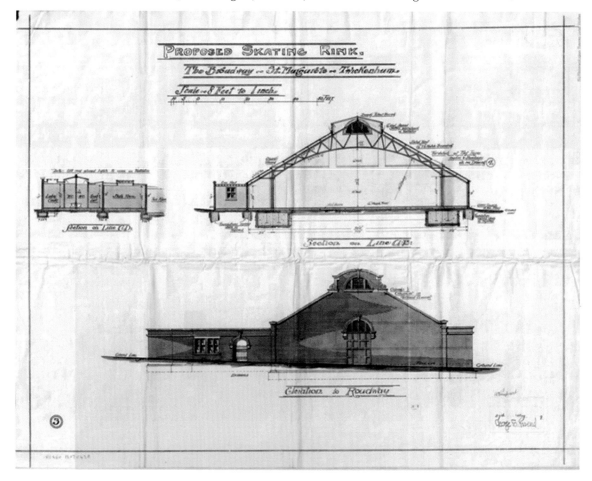

A similar advert in the *Thames Valley Times* carried an advertisement inviting applications for the purchase of eight thousand shares at £1 each, with projected profits of one hundred and twenty-five per cent. The prospectus stated:

> 'This Company has been formed for the purpose of acquiring and operating a properly equipped up-to-date Roller Skating Rink, situate close to the Terminus of the London United Tramway Co., Richmond Bridge in the parish of Twickenham. This is an excellent and suitable site for this purpose, in fact it would be impossible to find a better situation. The Rink practically adjoins the main road and will serve all the surrounding towns. It would be difficult to find a neighbourhood around London or elsewhere where a Skating Rink would appeal more to the inhabitants and those who frequent it for recreation – Richmond and pleasure are inseparable ... The revival of Roller Skating in England is phenomenal. This is mainly due to the greatly improved Ball Bearing Skates now in use and the improved floor surfaces ... making the pastime a health-giving, delightfully sociable and immensely enjoyable one. Roller skating is today the most popular indoor exercise ... this revival promises to be ... a permanent institution in this country, as in America.'

Unfortunately, Mr Bedworth's optimism and business acumen were ill-founded, as by 1912, all of his rinks had closed and the companies owning them had gone into liquidation. Work had started on constructing the Twickenham site between Clevedon Road and Cambridge Road, close to the terminus of London United Tramways Co. Ltd. The newspaper advertisement had stressed that the building would be made of brick, and thus serve as a valuable permanent asset, but sadly, only the shell had been constructed on the failure of the company. Investors lost their money, and the building stood empty until 1914.

Local resident Professor Jeremy Hamilton-Miller has documented much of the subsequent history of the site as part of his work for REIC (Richmond Environmental Information Centre, of which he is now patron), supported by Elaine Hooper, archivist at what is now The National Ice Skating Association of the United Kingdom (British Ice Skating): 'Shortly after the start of World War I, the Belgian entrepreneur Charles Pelabon set up his munitions factory on the site [see Chapter 17]. This remained in production until the end of the war in 1918. Other buildings were erected on the site during the war, all stipulated by the Council to be removed 'when peace arrives'. However ... in 1920, M. Pelabon asked not to be held to the original agreements to sell the land back within five years of hostilities having ceased, and he was given permission to change his type of production.

Eventually the Council, having made several concessions to M. Pelabon, started to press him to fulfil his obligations. At the same time, the East Twickenham Ratepayers Association became concerned over the continued use of the land for heavy industry. In February 1925 the Association formally complained to the Urban District Council (UDC) about the lack of action against M. Pelabon.

In reply, the UDC stated that it had earlier been "helpless to prevent it", for two reasons; first, the various restrictive agreements that had been made with M. Pelabon, second that he had returned to the Continent and could not be contacted. Shortly afterwards, M. Pelabon was asked to contribute £1,500 towards the construction of a pleasure ground (this had originally been suggested in 1919); he agreed to pay £1,250.

According to *Kelly's Directory* for 1925, the Pelabon Works had disappeared from the site, that was now occupied by other factories. At the end of 1925 the Council bought back their land for

£4,000. A counter offer from a manufacturer wishing to make "confectionery" was turned down.'

This research has been supplemented by local historian Dr Helen Baker, who advises that Charles Pelabon sold his land to local property developer Archibald Baird Craig in 1926. Press reports indicate that the site then ran as the Richmond Ice Rink Club, with public sessions in the evening, and was owned by a company from 1929 onwards of which Craig was managing director, with three others on the Board.

According to Professor Hamilton-Miller: 'In May 1928 a proposal made to adapt the former Pelabon Works as an ice-skating rink, under the management of the Richmond Ice Skating Rink Co., was agreed, and in December 1928 the ice rink was opened.

This was a spectacular affair, according to *[The] Richmond & Twickenham Times* of Dec[ember] 22: the ribbon was cut by Lady Hoare, wife of the Air Minister, in the presence of many local dignitaries and international skaters. Eight hundred skaters took to the ice "without the least suggestion of crowding".'

When it opened, it offered the longest stretch of ice in any indoor rink in the world, measuring 280 feet by 80 feet, providing room for one thousand skaters and three thousand spectators. It had a concrete barrel roof supported by concrete pillars and balconies. The rink was edged in mahogany and state-of-the-art ice-making machines were installed. It was to be used by several ice hockey teams.

Professor Hamilton-Miller continues: '... between 1 Jan[uary] and 15 May 1929 there were more than 20,000 visitors to the rink, and a profit of more than

£9,000 was reported. However, despite early enthusiasm, it is evident that this venture was not an unqualified success', perhaps because 'The rink was operated as a club (involving membership), rather than a place of entertainment for the general public.'

It closed on 31 May 1931, at the end of its usual season (October to May), after Fancy Dress on Ice and a New Year Carnival.

Professor Hamilton-Miller adds: '… when it reopened on 2 October [1931], with a civic ceremony, it was under entirely new management, and alterations had been made. It was also in future to be called "Richmond and Twickenham Ice Rink".' This new business appears to have closed in 1932.

How an Ice Rink Works (Richmond) – *Illustrated London News*, 22 March 1930 (By kind permission of *Illustrated London News*/Mary Evans Picture Library)

Dr Helen Baker's research suggests that between 1932 and 1934, the rink remained closed. Claude (or Charles) Langdon, who had developed the ice rink at the Palais de Danse in Hammersmith in 1929, raised the necessary money and then bought the site, some time around 1934. Press reports confirm the rink as having reopened in 1934, without mentioning Langdon's name; one story, however, refers to the adoption of the name Sportsdrome in 1934, which Langdon said he had invented. He recounts in his autobiography how, while planning to close his Hammersmith ice rink in 1934, he sailed past Richmond Ice Rink on a Hammersmith staff boat trip to Hampton Court, and was inspired to acquire and develop it.

Sometime after 1934, according to the Twickenham Museum website, new owners Major Hubert Martineau and the Rule family, made further changes: skaters and spectators were entertained by a resident orchestra, and seats at the south end of the rink were removed and replaced by a seawater pool. Water was brought up from the Sussex coast every week and the pool was kept warm using excess heat from the ice-making equipment. Unfortunately, the water was prone to going green with algae – and after a year, the pool was roofed over to create a more intimate ice rink. Skaters at the time were probably unaware that they were skating over a nine-foot void.

This smaller rink was named the 'Arosa' rink, reputedly after Arnold Gerschwiler's Swiss birthplace, although he was in fact born in Arbon, elsewhere in Switzerland.

The much reviled Joachim von Ribbentrop, German Ambassador to The Court of St James, reputedly bought a house next to the rink around 1936, apparently to indulge his passion for ice dancing. Coincidentally, he had lived in Arosa as a youth and one might speculate that he himself may have suggested the name for the new rink. During the war, he served as foreign minister under the Nazi regime, and was one of the first to be executed following the Nuremberg Trials for his war crimes.

Skating clubs that had previously been located at the rinks at Hammersmith and Earls Court transferred to Richmond, making it the premier rink in London. From the 1930s, the Aldwych Speed Club was based at Richmond, where it remained for some fifty-eight years until the rink finally closed its doors, when it moved to Guildford.

According to the Club's website: 'In the late 1940s through to the 1960s the club had backing of a very strong supporters club, some 600 strong at its peak. They used to have a permanent kiosk in the rink, selling programmes, photos, badges, etc. They used to organise coach trip[s] to away fixtures, social functions, and occasional financial assistance to the club. With so many names from the past, British Champions, record holders, and a few dozen candidates for the title of 'best skater ever to leave a championship'... Just

Arnold Gerschwiler, OBE, was born in Switzerland in 1914. Encouraged by his brother, Jacques, who was already an ice-skating instructor, he came to England. He competed in the British Open Championships in 1935 and 1936, and then became an instructor at Richmond in 1937. He was promoted to head coach a year later, running the tuition with Swiss precision, and taught until his retirement when the rink closed in 1992, interrupted only when the Swiss army called him up for a year in 1939.

Among the many professional skaters who benefited from his tuition were Valda Osborn (1953 European title holder), Ája Vrzáňová (world champion in 1949 and 1950), Sjoukje Dijkstra (winner of a string of Olympic and European titles in the 1960s), European, World and Olympic champion John Curry, and the British champions Michael Booker and Patricia Dodd.

Gerschwiler taught many celebrities, including Princess Anne, as well as film stars James Mason and Patricia Roc. The Richmond International Trophy, which ran from 1949 to 1980, was largely Gerschwiler's inspiration, as were the children's skating classes, started in 1949. He was made a director of the rink in 1964 and awarded an OBE in 1997. He and his wife Violet lived in Ailsa Road (north of Richmond Road and the A316) until his death in August 2003.

Aldwych Speed Club in the late 1930s
(Photo by permission of David King, whose father, Jack King, is on the extreme right of the back row)

about every British Championship and every British record, on both ice and rollers, has at some time or other been held by Aldwych members. As long ago as 1940 the roller side of the club was dropped and the club concentrated on ice speed.'

In 1939, at the outbreak of the Second World War, all theatres, halls and ice rinks were ordered to close. Since many American servicemen had skated and played ice hockey regularly at Richmond, the US Embassy persuaded the government to allow it to reopen, albeit with blacked-out windows.

David King, former local resident in Richmond Bridge Mansions, recalled his mother, Gwen Evans-King, a well-known ice dancer and teacher of the 1940s, dancing with Roy Callaway at Richmond. Roy was the husband of Betty Callaway, and both taught at Richmond Ice Rink. Betty was most famous as the coach of Jayne Torvill and Christopher Dean, ice dance champions in the 1984 Olympics; she also trained 1980 world champions Krisztina Regőczy and András Sallay, as well as 1972 European champions Angelika and Erich Buck.

While based at the Grosvenor House Hotel ice rink in Park Lane in the 1930s, two of Gwen's young pupils were a certain Elizabeth and Margaret Rose Windsor – the future Queen Elizabeth II and Princess Margaret.

David King remembers: 'From 1936–39 Gwen Evans-King was co-director of the international skating school at the Villars Palace Hotel in Villars-sur-Ollon, Vaud, Switzerland. Melitta Brunner, whom Gwen had met at the Westminster Ice Rink, was at the time the mistress of Hubert Martineau, who was a multi-millionaire and had formerly been one of the owners of Richmond Rink. Melitta was the instructress at the Palace Hotel in St Moritz before the war, and gave her job to Gwen Evans-King in 1946 as a result of their Westminster connection.'

David King's father, Jack King, was the manager of the NSA (National Skating Association) speed team. It was the NSA's tests that had previously established the formal tuition regime used at Richmond.

By 1945, the popular Sports-Drome (by now widely known as Richmond Ice Rink) was a large complex with an indoor golf range, and an outdoor bowling green, as well as two tennis courts, a pitch and putt course and a children's playground. Teas were served in the gardens fronting the river.

On 5 November 1951, the ice rink hosted an early television broadcast, declaring:

> 'There has, from time to time, been considerable controversy over television transmissions, but the Sports-Drome and its associated company Empress Hall (noted for its spectacular ice and stage productions) are pioneers in the field of anything progressive, convinced that the public, especially remotely resident, should have the opportunity of viewing everything of National interest. Ice skating today takes its place as possibly the greatest natural sport …'

Judging from the thousands of responses today from people who enjoyed skating at Richmond (and elsewhere), this may not be an overstatement.

The Arosa rink was also used as a film location, including for *The Man Between*, a 1953 British thriller starring James Mason and Claire Bloom.

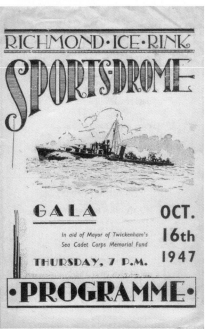

The ice rink as seen from the river in the 1950s (Richmond upon Thames Local Studies Library and Archive)

Far left: Richmond Ice Rink Gala souvenir programme, 1947 (Image provided by Kenneth Lea)

Left: A travelling entertainment show performing at Richmond Ice Rink, 1950 (Richmond upon Thames Local Studies Library and Archive)

Right: Richmond Ice Rink
souvenir programme, 1951
(Richmond upon Thames
Local Studies Library
and Archive)

Below: Ice Gala souvenir
programme, 1952
(Richmond upon Thames
Local Studies Library
and Archive)

Below right: Richmond
Trophy programme, 1975
(Richmond upon Thames
Local Studies Library
and Archive)

SOUVENIR PROGRAMME

TELEVISION TRANSMISSION from the RICHMOND ICE RINK

Tonight we have the pleasure of part of this evening's proceedings being televised and we would ask your indulgence during that period by observing the requests which may be made over the Public Address system regarding applause, etc.

There has, from time to time, been considerable controversy over television transmission, but the Sports-Drome and its associated company Empress Hall (noted for its spectacular ice and stage productions) are pioneers in the field of anything progressive, convinced that the public, especially remotely resident, should have the opportunity of viewing everything of National interest. Ice skating today takes its place as possibly the greatest natural sport contributing towards improved health and physical fitness besides being a pleasing recreation and offering an opening for a well-paid career.

5th NOV. 1951

SPORTS-DROME

SPORTS-DROME THE ICE RINK RICHMOND BRIDGE

In connection with Borough of TWICKENHAM

Presents The Season's Opening

FAIR

ICE GALA

on SATURDAY — SEPTEMBER 6TH 1952 AT SEVEN

SOUVENIR PROGRAMME

The Richmond Trophy

MONDAY 3rd November, 1975

Programme

Professional ice dance teachers Anne and Roy Lee were amongst those coaching at Richmond Ice Rink, which was fast becoming world-famous. Several members of the royal family, such as Princess Anne, Prince Andrew and the Earl of Snowdon (then Viscount Linley), were also taught at Richmond.

British, European, Olympic and world champions Jayne Torvill and Christopher Dean trained at Richmond Rink in the 1970s and 1980s, as did Robin Cousins, another Olympic and European champion, world medallist (1978–1980) and British champion (1977–1980). John Curry, 1976 Olympic and World Champion, makes up the group of title holders who remember the rink with fondness, and subsequently enjoyed (or still enjoy) glittering careers in the entertainment industry. Even Margaret Thatcher, British Prime Minister from 1979 to 1990, came to the rink to watch them.

This exalted history explains why Richmond Ice Rink, often considered as the spiritual home of British ice-skating, became something of a legend within the Borough of Richmond upon Thames and the wider area. The rink was at the heart of a community where children grew up and socialised, and where many met their future partners, such as Anne and Roy Lee themselves. Today, hundreds of people write on social media with affection and passion about their experiences in and around the rink, sharing photos and memories.

Devastating for so many, the rink was to close in 1992, but skaters from

There are innumerable stories from the six decades when the ice rink was entertaining thousands of skaters, young and old. One perhaps not captured elsewhere is that of Mary Groombridge (pictured here, fifth from right), a British ice-skating champion who later became a judge at Richmond and elsewhere in the UK and France.

She may have been somewhat of a maverick by nature, someone with a real passion for her sport, reputedly voting for whom she saw as the best skater on the day, rather than for whoever's turn it was to win. Perhaps this explains why she was banned for a period as a judge.

David Daines, who photographed the very last days of the ice rink, reported that 'Mary was scrupulously fair in judging tests and competitions. She was known for giving wonderfully helpful advice to any skater [for whom] she unfortunately felt she had to fail a test... when she was young she was warned that her health was delicate and she would live long only by not taking any strenuous activities. Typical Mary, she completely disregarded this and skated and skied well into old age. Mary though would never suffer fools, not at all. It was a privilege to know her.'

Mary knew the British artist Vernon Ward (1905–1985) in WWII, when he was helping maintain ambulances for the Civil Defence Service in Richmond, and became his PA for nearly fifty years until his death. Trained at the Slade School of Fine Art, he was the subject of a book by author and artist Josephine Walpole, *Vernon Ward: Child of the Edwardian Era* (Antique Collectors' Club, 1988) for which Mary provided most of the stories.

Some sources suggest that Vernon Ward painted a symbolic figure composition for the Free French during WWII, and designed the naval plaque for the War Memorial in Radnor Gardens, Twickenham. Sadly, the signature is no longer present to confirm this, since the original was stolen in 2011, and had to be replaced from photos.

Mary knew the Calloways and many other well-known skaters and instructors of her time. She later had a skating award named after her: the Mary Groombridge Friendship Trophy, still being awarded in 2015.

Right: A young Mary Groombridge, seen here fifth from the right, in the RAISC Dance Team, March 1956 (Photo from the Mary Groombridge estate)

Richmond continued to meet regularly, particularly the members of the Richmond Flyers (formerly the Phoenix Flyers), an ice hockey team.

The demise of the ice rink was contentious, and still provokes strong emotions in people today. Residents' distrust of local authority agreements with private companies, just as much a theme in public life as in Henry Cresswell Foulkes' day, grew when Richmond Borough in 1988 granted permission to the London & Edinburgh Trust, then owners of the rink, to demolish the site and build a gated development of luxury flats and town houses by the river. A year later, instead of forcing the company to plan for a new rink, the borough apparently accepted a fee of £2.5 million and removed the stipulation.

A petition was raised to prevent the rink's closure, and people marched to No. 10 Downing Street in 1990. The following decade was plagued by allegations of council corruption, mismanagement and incompetence, accompanied by ombudsman and audit enquiries, legal cases and investigative journalism.

The UK Parliament website records an early day motion tabled five years later, on 16 January 1995:

> 'That this House is deeply concerned about the circumstances that led to the closure of Richmond Ice Rink, a world famous sports facility, by Richmond upon Thames Council; notes the campaign that was launched by Mr Richard Meacock which has led to this matter being considered by the European Court; congratulates the Richmond and Twickenham Times in which an editorial dated 13 January 1995 questioned the lack of progress in securing a new ice rink facility in the borough; commends the excellent efforts of Councillor Michael Gold and Councillor Liz Mackenzie in exposing this matter; and calls on the Secretary of State for the Environment to initiate an immediate public inquiry into this entire matter so that the truth of what has happened can be explained to all interested parties.'

J M Lee reported in *The Making of Modern Twickenham* that 'Twickenham suspicions were also increased by the support given to Richmond Museum by the London & Edinburgh Trust. This company's generosity was extended to purchasing the painting by Peter Tillemans called *A Prospect of Twickenham* (c.1725) when the council was outbid at the auction. But instead of allowing local people to see the picture displayed, as it had promised, the company sold it on'. Also known as *The Prospect of the River Thames at Twickenham*, a panoramic view of Twickenham from across the river, it is happily now part of Richmond Borough Art Collection.

The doors of the ice rink were finally closed in January 1992 and the building demolished shortly afterwards. The new Richmond Bridge Estate development which replaced it is described by estate agents as a 'landmark' gated development of luxury apartments with 24-hour concierge service, residents' gyms and attractive communal gardens.

In late 2014, a project was established by the Richmond Environmental Information Centre (REIC), with a grant from the Heritage Lottery Fund, to give local people the opportunity to record memories and lend photographs and other memorabilia about the ice rink.

Berkley Driscoll and Teresa Read, two trustees of REIC, were behind the independent company, Twickenham Alive (Ice Rink), with the aim of bringing back ice skating to Twickenham: this company

The Amateur
Figure Skating Championships
of Great Britain

RICHMOND
DEC. 1969

ran three temporary community ice rinks during the life of the project, the first at York House and the second two at Strawberry Hill House.

These rinks were initially staffed by those who had grown up skating in East Twickenham, and managed by an international ice hockey player who has been honoured in the Ice Hockey Hall of Fame. The same Zamboni (ice resurfacing) operator who had worked at Richmond Rink tended the ice. The temporary rink was visited by many local skaters, and even the well-remembered ticket collector from the Richmond Rink.

The project established a stall in the skate exchange at the Strawberry Hill House rink over the Christmas and New Year period in 2014, to make contact with potential contributors and gather information. Following enthusiastic response, a day's filming was set up to record their interviews. One lady who had started working at the rink in 1949 recounted 'working at the rink for half of her life starting in administration and ending up as a Director of the rink, being one of the last people to leave the rink when it closed in 1992'.

The contributors included hockey players, dancers, figure skaters, professional teachers and pupils who had attended the children's Saturday morning lessons. In the follow-ups, more skating friends and memories and photographs emerged, and yet more filmed interviews.

The ice rink viewed from the Richmond side of the river (Image provided by the Mary Groombridge estate)

The interior of the ice rink (Richmond upon Thames Local Studies Library and Archive)

Support from Elaine Hooper, archivist and historian of the National Ice Skating Association (NISA), included five years' of diaries of one of the campaigners to bring a new ice rink back to the borough, the late Richard Meacock. There is a personal account online from Richard Meacock, written before his death in 2006, which recounts his thirteen-year battle to preserve or replace the Richmond Ice Rink, and of the administrative and legal shenanigans involving the borough, developers, politicians, the media, police and others (icerinx.com/meacock).

A local school whose pupils enjoyed ice skating at the temporary rink at Strawberry Hill House agreed to participate; older students were involved in filming and editing a promotional video for the project website, to attract more participants to the project.

Cheryl Nolan, who had skated at the rink in 1979, left this memory at the skate exchange: 'Ice skating was a PE option at my Richmond school; last session on a Friday afternoon, terrific fun and great socially. It's where I learnt to skate – a beautiful building which I didn't appreciate at the time.'

The project team had been impressed by the Torvill and Dean project 'Ice Rink on the Estate' and worked successfully with the temporary ice rink at Strawberry Hill House to provide a club for school children to bring ice skating back to the borough as a sport.

Work began compiling the memories of skaters for a book, for which Jayne Torvill and Christopher Dean agreed to write the introduction: *The Most Famous Ice Rink in the World*. Many local residents, who had been children, teenagers, ice hockey players and ice skating coaches over many years at Richmond Rink, added memories from the 1930s until its closure in 1992. Some came from families with a history of two or three generations at the rink.

Soon after the opening of the temporary ice rink at Strawberry Hill House at Christmas 2015, the REIC opened its first exhibition at the skate exchange there, with copies of the book on show: over seven weeks it was seen by people of all ages. Dennis Gilbert, a well-known portrait painter and former President of the Contemporary Portrait Society, who had sketched at Richmond Ice Rink in 1956, came along to the rink to once again sketch the skaters.

Another legacy was the project work archived by the National Ice Skating Association (NISA) as well as Richmond Local Studies Library and Archive. A number of videos of skating at Richmond Rink were acquired and donated to the

One of the information boards by the former Ice Rink site (Source: REIC Heritage Lottery Fund project The Most Famous Ice Rink in the World)

archive at NISA, including a skating performance and practice session featuring Jayne Torvill and Christopher Dean in 1984.

Professor Jeremy Hamilton-Miller, patron of REIC, wrote at the time: 'Although the Ice Rink closed almost 25 years ago, its memory has lingered on in the Borough. So we were quietly confident at the outset that this project would yield fruit. In the event, the response to Memories was almost overwhelming at times. Some of the stories were touching, funny, of genuine historical interest or, occasionally, sad. The book we produced could have been filled at least twice over with reminiscences. A truly remarkable new archive has been created, that will enable a better understanding of why the Rink continues to be held in such affection.

… A question remains, however: why was it called Richmond Ice Rink? It is in the geographical confines of Twickenham, was granted planning permission by the newly fledged Borough of Twickenham (succeeding the previous Urban District Council), and in 1932 the Council approved the name 'Richmond and Twickenham Skating Rink'. However, clearly this was not formally adopted. Thus the name remained Richmond Ice Rink; the memory lives on, now much enhanced and given new life by the present project, in which I was proud to have been a minor player.'

In 2017, the East Twickenham Centennial Group installed a memorial on the riverside by the former Ice Rink site commemorating the East Twickenham Belgian story from WWI (see Chapter 17). Two information boards remain for the public, depicting the Belgian story and the transformation of the riverside Works building into The Sports-Drome, later to become Richmond Ice Rink. These were designed and produced by the independent 'social enterprise' company Twickenham Alive (of which Berkley Driscoll and Teresa Read are directors), with contributions from Professor Hamilton-Miller. Berkley Driscoll and Teresa Read continue to work closely with Professor Hamilton-Miller as chairman and secretary, respectively, of REIC.

Richmond Rink was much loved and is part of ice-skating history, as well as the history of East Twickenham. It may well be the best-loved ice rink in the world, as well as being named 'The Most Famous Ice Rink in the World' (in the words of David Daines, a member of the ice dance club). And today, people still campaign for a new rink. On 19 May 2020, during the Covid-19 pandemic, this was one plea on social media:

> 'We were promised a new ice rink, time has come for it to happen. We as a country need projects like this to restart our country. It's a good time for renewing our thoughts, maybe we can build kindness, togetherness and teamwork. I would have given up on life if I hadn't had the family vibes from Richmond Ice Rink. I have been to many rinks and none have made me feel so safe/at home.'

CHAPTER 20

PICTURE PALACE TO BILLIARD HALL

In addition to the attractions over the bridge in Richmond, off-duty excitements in the early twentieth century in East Twickenham were on offer at the Grand Picture Theatre, which opened on the north side of Richmond Road in 1912. The following year it was renamed the Gaiety Picture Playhouse, but by 1931 it had become a Temperance Billiard Hall, and today is offices at Nos. 417–421 Richmond Road.

The rocky road of this cinema was as volatile as anything one might imagine in the film world: the turbulent tale features stars stepping down from the silver screen to take control of the business, along with people from all walks of life, even grocers, diversifying into bringing entertainment to the people. Thanks to Twickenham Park Residents Association's investigations, the story of this precarious venture has recently come under the spotlight.

Plans by Walter Charles Phillips of Kingston for the proposed Picture Theatre on Richmond Road, 1910 (Richmond upon Thames Local Studies Library and Archive)

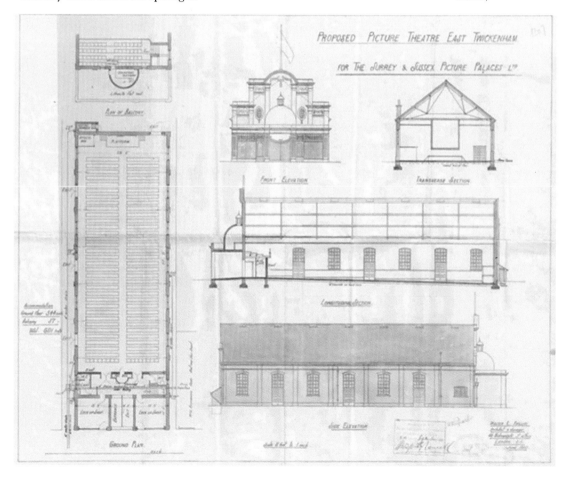

The first plans for a picture house in the neighbourhood were conceived by the newly formed Surrey and Sussex Picture Palaces Ltd. who had purchased the site of the former Spring Lodge in Richmond Road, a recently demolished villa from 1830.

Surrey and Sussex Picture Palaces had already opened two theatres in Kingston and Merton. The Richmond Road site was set to be the third but the company's rapid growth brought financial difficulties and the forced sale of all their assets by 1912.

Unfortunately for East Twickenham, the picture house was not yet complete when Surrey and Sussex Picture Palaces ceased operations. The original plans by architect Walter Charles Phillips of Kingston show an elaborate entrance foyer, which never came into being.

A new owner for the partly constructed picture house was found by 1911, and a fresh architect, Mr Clarke Ashworth of Richmond, was commissioned to finish the theatre.

The Gaiety Picture Playhouse opened on Saturday 2 March 1912. Contemporary press articles show that the management was under Mr L Courlander who was also associated with the nearby Castle Theatre in Richmond; he was the manager of The Castle Cine Syndicate which ran both venues.

Postcard from 1915, showing Richmond Road towards the bridge and the Gaiety Picture Palace on the left
(Postcard image provided by Alan Winter)

On the day of its opening, the *Richmond & Twickenham Times* described the venue:

'... considerable care and thought has been devoted to making it one of the most comfortable and up-to-date picture palaces in the neighbourhood. Lounge and writing rooms have been provided off the entrance hall, and

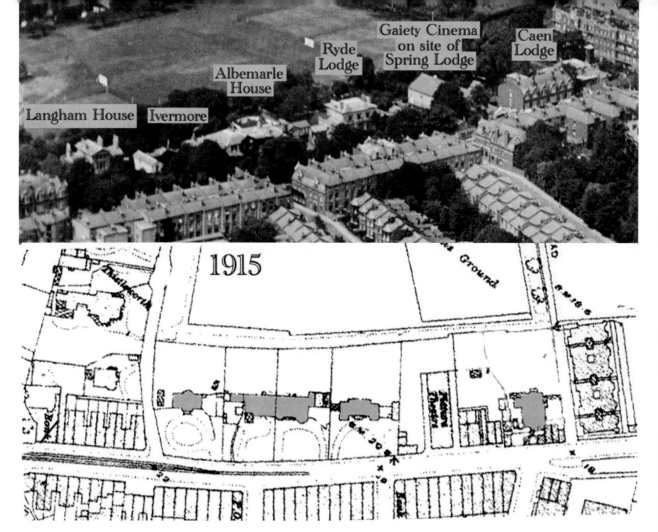

Langham House   Ivermore   Albemarle House   Ryde Lodge   Gaiety Cinema on site of Spring Lodge   Caen Lodge

1915

the theatre itself, which seats six hundred, has a raise which assures for everyone a clear view of the screen. The latest type of cinematograph machines, electrically driven to ensure steadiness, have been installed ... A very handsome frontage has been designed ... Corinthian pillars and capitals with pilasters and decorative panels, in semi-circular recessed front and marble mosaic pavement, add to the external appearance, and the theatre itself has been richly decorated with mural panels, after the style of Watteau. These are illuminated by concealed lights.'

The Gaiety Picture Playhouse changed its name in November 1913 to The Gaiety Picture Palace, a name which continued into 1914.

The management changed several times in 1915. The two rate book extracts from that year show the occupier as Thomas Cavill Vince, owner of a variety agency for actors in London. He is listed in the book for April, but by October has been replaced by H Ambrose Ltd. By the end of November, the theatre had been completely redecorated, 'fitted with modern heating apparatus' and with 'High class music ... introduced into the programme'.

Above: The photo and map show the location in Richmond Road of the Albert Cinema in 1915, together with the other large houses on the north side at the time.
(All photos and images in this chapter from Twickenham Park Residents Association unless otherwise stated)

Richmond and Twickenham Times

A JOURNAL OF LOCAL NEWS, SOCIETY, ART, AND LITERATURE.

Circulating in Richmond, Kingston, Surbiton, Norbiton, Twickenham, Brentford, Hounslow, Chiswick (Turnham Green, Bedford Park, Gunnersbury), Mortlake, Barnes, Ham, Petersham, Isleworth, Putney, Kew, and Teddington.

SATURDAY, JUNE 17, 1916.

GAIETY CINEMA,

TWICKENHAM (foot of Richmond Bridge).

Manager · · · · · · Mr. A. RAMSDEN.

GRAND RE-OPENING

On Wednesday, June 21st, 1916

(QUEEN ALEXANDRA'S ROSE DAY)

MR. HORATIO BOTTOMLEY (Editor, "John Bull").

Has promised to be present on this occasion and will address the visitors.

To the Opening Ceremony and the Afternoon Performance only guests of the Management will be admitted by invitation card.

Grand Re-opening to the Public at 7 p.m.

FULL PROGRAMME. ORCHESTRA. POPULAR PRICES.

FEATURES:

1. VIA WIRELESS. Pathe's Thriller.
    A film you will never forget. See the blowing up of a beautifully appointed luxury yacht in mid-ocean, the bursting of a big gun, and the hurling of an expensive motor car over the precipitous cliffs to be dashed to powder.

2. MARY PICKFORD in "THE UNWELCOME GUEST." The highest salaried film artist at her best.

3–5. Three other films which are funny without being vulgar.

6. Topical Budget—and a Surprise!

Get the "Gaiety News," giving the full programme. Sent post free on application to the Manager.

The **Entire Receipts** on the Opening Day will be handed over, without any deduction, to the **War Seal Foundation**, Mr Stoll's excellent scheme for housing our Disabled Heroes after the War.

Now named the Albert Hall ('chosen out of compliment to the gallant King of the Belgians'), this was soon changed to the Albert Cinema, and was at this time largely focussed on serving the local Belgian community associated with the WWI Pelabon munitions works.

The proprietor H Ambrose continued through into 1916, with the local directory showing one of the company directors as Colette Olga Touzeau, presumably Belgian herself, who lived nearby in St Margarets Road.

Following the name change to the Albert Cinema, the theatre then returned as the Gaiety Cinema, reopening in June 1916. The manager was Mr A Ramsden, formerly of the Teddington Picture House. The cinema was duly redecorated.

The grand reopening featured Horatio Bottomley (1860–1933), who was an English financier, journalist, editor, newspaper proprietor and Member of Parliament. Co-founder of the *Financial Times*, he was editor of the popular magazine *John Bull*, and lauded for his patriotic oratory during World War I.

Bottomley spoke in support of the War Seal Foundation, established by Sir Oswald Stoll to provide 'a place to call home' and vital support for injured war veterans and their families.

Miss Dorothy Bellew,
film actor
(© National Portrait
Gallery, London)

Bottomley's later activities, however, sadly led to him being convicted of fraud and sentenced to seven years' imprisonment in 1922.

In 1917, the actor Miss Dorothy Bellew (1891–1973) became the proprietor. She appeared in around sixty films during the silent era, including the title role in *Lorna Doone* in 1912, in *Hard Times* (1915) and *The Convent Gate* (1913).

Born Dorothy Falck, and sister to stage and film actor Kyrle Bellew, she married Mr Stephen Slinger, a theatre manager, in 1920. Following her marriage, she and her husband were associated with a number of picture houses, including establishments in Chelmsford and Epping.

Films shown under her direction included *The Clodhopper*, a comedy drama from 1917, and *Souls Triumphant* with Lilian Gish in the same year. Advertising described the cinema as 'Under Entirely New and Capable Management'.

According to *The Sketch* of 29 May 1918, the cinema was 'prospering vastly, despite the fact that on the opening day the light failed, and she had to apologise and return heaps of money to her patrons … She has a bevy of beautiful girls as her assistants, and on Whit Monday, despite the war's delays, she arranged for all of them to appear in their new uniform of white linen faced with pink'.

As with many of its other owners, though, her time at the Gaiety appears to have been short-lived.

Following Dorothy Bellew's tenure, the Gaiety once more changed hands: it next became the New Gaiety Cinema, but the business remained beset by technical and staffing problems.

The management advertised for a relief pianist who 'must be very fond of music, fond of films, and must be prepared to take unceasing pains to adapt the music to the film … Our chief pianist is known as the best cinema pianist in West and South-west London; but if we are to make the Gaiety the Perfect Cinema that we HOPE it will be, we must have more music.'

On 26 October 1918, Gaiety Gossip reported in the *Richmond & Twickenham Times*:

> 'Terrible Troubles we've been having! Really, no-one not in the business can know how many things can go wrong in a cinema.

> During the last few weeks it's been operating – we believe in employing wounded soldiers, and he's had some hard luck – for which he and we apologise to our friends.

> But thank goodness that's all right now, and we all (including Cox, operator) hope that you'll pour in next week to enjoy our good show and our good operating. Will you?'

In the following week (2 November 1918) the *Richmond & Twickenham Times* continued the story:

> 'The management of the New Gaiety has had some trouble with the lantern, which has not been doing good work lately. They have succeeded in overcoming many difficulties, and the pictures are now showing in a proper manner.'

The reports of November 1918 also reference the 1918–1919 influenza pandemic which decimated populations around the world, a century before the Covid-19 pandemic:

'The management is closing for an hour between 6 and 7 every evening to enable the hall to be disinfected.'

Many of the comments echo similar experiences in the UK and elsewhere in 2020 to 2021, as Gaiety Gossip in the *Richmond & Twickenham Times* reported on 2 November 1918:

'This influenza has been hard on us down here. We kept the Gaiety well aired and open as usual because we were informed that it was best for the public to have a warm cheerful place to which it could go – but you would be astounded to know how much money we've lost in these two weeks. Hope we do well next week!'

The management's pleas to potential audiences were unrelenting: 'Noticed our improved operating? Just about the clearest pictures in the district now. Besides, Cox got in a new machine from Kam's and we've had the electricians in, so we're all ready to give you a good show next week. Which day, please?'

Managers continued to change during the influenza pandemic. An advert from 7 December 1918 mentions that Mr Vincent, 'another wounded soldier', had taken over the position of manager from Mrs Lomas.

And so did the operators: '... we ... got one of their very best men, with a good practical experience – F. Oliver. He can't walk very well, but he certainly can show a fine picture.'

Aerial shot of Richmond Road, c.1919. The Gaiety Cinema hall is centre left.

1919 brought another change of proprietor, Mrs Madgley, and by February, she had brought in new management under Quality Kinema Ltd., with lessees Lewis Sidney Darling and Gordon Quick. The business venture between managers Quick and Darling was of short duration. Darling had been connected with the Premier Electric Theatre in Earlsfield, Wandsworth; he had married Florence Smith of the Bijou Theatre in South Street, Isleworth, in 1912. Gordon Quick (described by the press as 'the enterprising manager of the Gaiety Cinema') soon left the business, and Darling and his wife moved to the New Pavilion Cinema in Richmond before finally relocating to Kent. Mrs Madgley was presumably disappointed in her high hopes for the business.

By July 1919, new proprietor William Collinson was in place at the Gaiety, 'a gentleman with nearly twenty years' experience', who once more smartened up the seven-year-old premises. Like several of those who came before, his time too was limited: he left in 1920 to take over the Palace Cinema in Walton-on-Thames, later renamed the Regent Cinema.

By mid-1920, a new manager, H A Warren, was in place.

In 1921, the Gaiety showed a film entitled *The Auction of Souls* which had not been certified by The British Board of Film Censors (BBFC). This resulted in the latest owners, Dubowski and Michaels, being taken to court by the local authority, Middlesex County Council, who lost the case as well as the subsequent appeal. The Lord Chief Justice decided that 'the Council had no right to delegate its powers to such an arbitrary authority' as the BBFC.

Right, top: Poster for the film *Auction of Souls*, which landed the owners of the Gaiety in court for showing an uncertified film

Right, below: Live boxing was shown twice nightly in April 1925 before the big feature – a film about boxing

THE RICHMOND AND TWICKENHAM TIMES
SATURDAY, NOVEMBER 20, 1920.

Abraham Dubowski and Michael Michaels were a partnership of two East London grocers who were brothers-in-law and had taken the bold step of running the cinema.

It appears that Michaels subsequently left the business, perhaps to return to the safer world of fruit and veg: the Twickenham Council rate book of October 1921 now shows Dubowski as sole proprietor of the Gaiety.

The cinema operation was fast becoming a spectacle in its own right: 1922 brought yet another change of management, with the advent of Middlesex Kinemas, under proprietor Alec Hyman Blackman. This business was established by the Blackman family of Whitechapel, London, with Philip Blackman and his son Alec as principal directors.

After yet another redecoration, Blackman at last turned the fortunes of The New Gaiety by incorporating live vaudeville acts to cheer the audience between silent films with exciting titles such as *The Queen of Sheba* (1921) and *While the Devil Laughs* (1921), featuring actor Louise Lovely. Another film was *The Playhouse* (1921), written, directed by and starring Buster Keaton, who played every role in the first sequence of this twenty-three-minute film.

In 1924, the big screen showed *The Hunchback of Notre Dame* (1923), which was enhanced by an 'Augmented Orchestra', 'Vocal Prologue' and 'Stage Effects'. Another film, *The Temple of Venus* (1923), featured Mary Philbin, a last-minute stand-in for Jean Arthur, who had been fired after the director became dissatisfied with her performance; it also featured '1,000 American Beauties'.

The Gaiety now diversified again, showing live boxing for a short time in 1925, but offering 'a film mainly for women' the following week.

At this point, however, Blackman, the manager, was fined £37 10s and two guineas costs for a tax irregularity concerning an untorn cinema ticket kept among receipts – which 'might be used again', as reported, a little bizarrely, in a Scottish newspaper, the *Evening Telegraph and Post* of Dundee.

The Gaiety's closest competitor at the time was The Lyric Cinema, at the Twickenham end of Richmond Road.

Advertisements showed the New Gaiety and Lyric Cinema, together with the Teddington Picture and Vaudeville House, which were also managed by Middlesex Kinemas.

Variety acts continued to feature during this run of success, such as 'Desmond Kelvin, the Successful Baritone' and 'Reg. Graham, Versatile Light Comedian and Speciality Dancer. Character dances including Hunting, Scarecrow, Hornpipe, Legmania, Dutch, Soft Shoe'.

Films shown included WWI title *Ypres (Wipers)* from 1925, and *Never The Twain Shall Meet*, from the same year, by French director Maurice Tourneur, offering free packs of Lyons Tea to audience members.

The venue was again renamed, this time as the New Gaiety Kinema, matching the name of the parent business, showing films like *A Little Girl In A Big City* of 1925, which was 'Adults Only Admitted': the main character was played by Gladys Walton, real-life love interest of contemporary gangster Al Capone. It was her last role before being fired by Universal Studios for violation of the morality clause in her contract.

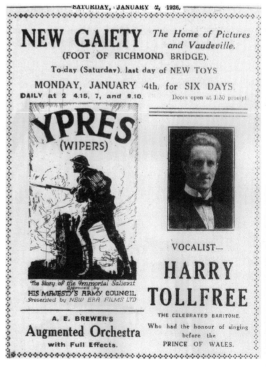

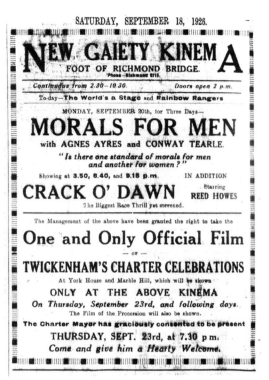

The success of the business in its current form was apparently recognised when it helped celebrate Twickenham's new standing as a Municipal Borough in 1926, with permission to produce and show the 'One and Only Official Film' of the Charter Celebrations.

Its showing was attended by the Charter Mayor.

In 1927, another risk for the industry was highlighted when a fire destroyed 29,000 feet of celluloid on its way to the sister venue in Teddington. The driver and passengers managed to throw another 14,000 feet of film stock on to the road before the lorry became a 'roaring furnace'. All over in ten minutes, this was 'A Film Thrill' (as the *Evening News* and *Southern Daily Mail* of 11 March 1927 reported it) of a very different sort.

The Kinema continued to show some high-profile silent films, such as *Mare Nostrum*, a 1926 silent film directed by Irish producer and director Rex Ingram and starring his wife, Alice Terry. Set during World War I, the film follows a Spanish merchant sailor who becomes involved with a spy, promising 'A Colossal Attraction'.

Its billing included the intriguing line, 'The Spy System is so truthfully exposed in this Drama, that the German Government made a Request to withdraw it from Exhibition in this Country.'

The Gaiety Kinema is listed in the two *Kinematograph Year Books* for 1927 and 1928, along with Blackman's other venues in Teddington, Hampton and Wandsworth.

By 1928, Blackman was expanding his management team to include a publicity and vaudeville manager.

An advert from that year shows the Gaiety Kinema with its usual mix of silent films and variety acts – including more listed with 'Adults Only' content.

Twickenham's latest cinema, the New Kinema De Luxe, had just opened opposite York House, directly next door to The Lyric. Being much larger and with far better facilities, The Lyric's future was becoming doubtful.

By 1929, the Gaiety itself was losing out to nearby competition, and had installed equipment for the audience to experience the new talkies.

Nonetheless, larger purpose-built cinemas had recently been built in Richmond as well as Twickenham. Despite showing hits such as *Show Boat* in 1929, the business, with Simon Blackman as chairman, went into voluntary liquidation in January 1930.

TRADES DIRECTORY, 1952.

BILLIARD ROOMS.

Temperance Billiard Halls Ltd.

TEMPERANCE

Tel. MACaulay 3960.

BILLIARD HALLS Ltd.

HEAD OFFICE; 638-640 WANDSWORTH ROAD, S.W.8.

Acton, 27 King street W3
Battersea, 66 Battersea rise SW11
Brentford, York house, Great West road
Chelsea, 131 King's road SW3
Croydon, 16 Katherine street
Ealing, 34/42 Bond street W5
Hammersmith, 150 King street W6
Highbury, 12 Highbury corner N5
Hounslow, 1 High street
Ilford, 257 High road
Kingston, 17-19 Fife road
Lewisham, 237 High street SE13
Putney, 118 High street SW15
Richmond, Red Lion street
St. Margaret's, 423 Richmond road
Streatham, 42 Streatham High road
  SW16
Tooting, 8 Mitcham road SW17
Twickenham, 1-3 Richmond road
Victoria, 104-112 Buckingham palace
  road SW1
Wimbledon, 111 The Broadway SW19
Wood Green, 1-3 High road N15
Worthing, 12 Bath place

In 1930, the Electoral Register for the cinema shows Alex Blackman's brother Simon and his wife Katie Dubowski. They married in 1931, Katie being the daughter of Asher Dubowski, a grocer in East London. He was directly related to Abraham Dubowski who with his business partner Michael Michaels had operated The Gaiety in 1921.

By 28 March 1930, the doors had closed and the contents of the cinema were auctioned. The Gaiety and its old competitor, The Lyric in Twickenham, were both now closed as picture houses and sold independently. The Gaiety and Lyric had been constructed around the same time and internally were very similar. More akin to a village hall in design, they were often referred to as 'fleapits' and were unable to match the plush modern amenities and state-of-the-art technology on offer elsewhere.

Both properties were converted into billiard halls by Temperance Billiard Halls Ltd., a successful company offering alcohol-free entertainment, which had initially constructed attractive public rooms in Manchester and the surrounding area, before moving to London.

The initials of the
Temperance Billiard Hall
are still visible in the tiled
mosaic floor of the inner
foyer today.

The Gaiety now became known as the St Margarets Temperance Billiard Hall, and the 1952 London Trades Directory shows similar billiard halls in the vicinity.

The foyer of the Gaiety was refashioned to suit and remained largely unchanged until the billiard hall finally shut its doors in around 1954.

In 1955, a planning application was put forward to employ the former cinema and billiard hall as a factory for assembling plastic toys.

Temperance Billiard Halls Ltd. eventually sold off the last of its sites in 1964.

In 1964, the Tony Lane licensed betting shop occupied the building's left-hand shop facing the road (see Chapter 23). The other shop, which for many years had been the Gaiety Snack Bar, now became an estate agent.

A proposal was rejected in 1983 to erect a four-storey office building on the site. Instead, an extension was raised above the foyer and the property now became known as Richmond Bridge House. Today it is used as serviced office accommodation, while the remaining one-storey hall still projects out to the rear, used as an MOT centre.

Like Richmond and Petersham on the other bank of the Thames, East Twickenham still attracts many names from the worlds of television, cinema and theatre as residents today. Some one hundred years after a local picture palace first drew in crowds from the new suburban population, the community must now cross the bridge or head further afield for large-screen or stage entertainment. Today's easy transport links into and out of the area evolved throughout the twentieth century from horse-drawn carriages and trams to electric cars and buses. That evolution too was not straightforward.

Richmond Bridge House today, formerly the Gaiety Cinema in its various incarnations and then the Temperance Billiard Hall (Photo by Jonathan Crofts)

CHAPTER 21
BUSES, TRAMS AND AUTOMOBILES

In nineteenth-century London, the expansion of the steam railway system brought outlying areas within easy reach of the city, and with it, builders eagerly in search of land suitable for development.

In 1846, the London & South Western Railway introduced a line from Nine Elms to terminate at Richmond. Two years later, the line was extended to Windsor, via Twickenham, and with the provision of these two stations, Richmond and Twickenham immediately became attractive to families wishing to leave the smoke-ridden capital for a rural and more healthy environment.

Life was pleasant in this leafy suburb but the lack of local public transport was keenly felt. It was a considerable distance between the railway stations of Richmond and Twickenham, with no ready means of passing between the two other than on foot. A hansom cab from Richmond Station was expensive, as much as 2s.0d. to some parts of St Margarets, and cycling technology was as yet in its infancy and not risked by many, save for the most daring of young gentlemen.

In 1873, representation was made to the London & South Western Railway by a body of gentlemen residents of Cambridge Park, Twickenham Park and St Margarets (including Henry Little, the Cambridge Park developer) for the provision of an intermediate stop between the two stations. The railway company proved extremely reluctant to accept this suggestion. Meetings were held in the Montpelier School in Orleans Road, and it was pointed out to the company that the cost would not be excessive, as 'there was no need for new rails, engines or carriages, nor an extra guard or engineer. All that would be required would be the employment of a stationmaster at £3 per week, three porters at 30s. each and a booking clerk at £2 per week'. After nearly three years' of discussion, the day was won and building began on the new railway station to be known as St Margarets, which was opened in 1876.

Recognising the potential of this expanding commuter suburb, the Brentford, Isleworth & Twickenham Tramways promoted a Bill in Parliament in 1878 for a tramline to run between Kew Bridge, Brentford, Isleworth and St Margarets, terminating in East Twickenham at the foot of Richmond Bridge. When the Bill came before the Commons, the solicitor for Lady Chichester, then owner of Cambridge House, stated that it would be 'Intolerable to have the ragtag and bobtail disgorged before her Ladyship's lodge', and the St Margarets section was removed from the scheme. It was another twenty-five years before a tramway system finally came through to East Twickenham in 1903.

Tolls had been removed on Richmond Bridge in 1859, whereupon East Twickenham had become a sort of 'West Richmond'. Tensions between its residents and those of the rest of Twickenham were reinforced by a growing sense of their own identity, with the creation of their own parish of St Stephen's in 1875 (see Chapter 14), and their own station a year later at St Margarets. Many also chose to shop at the wider selection in Richmond, rather than in the perhaps more humble emporiums of central Twickenham, prior to the arrival of Henry Foulkes' parade of shops leading up to the bridge.

As J M Lee commented in *The Making of Modern Twickenham*:

> 'Twickenham seemed to have enjoyed an Indian summer of graceful living in the 1880s and 1890s before the winter of suburban monotony set in. Lady Peel was in residence in Marble Hill House until her death in 1887. She was thoroughly familiar with East Twickenham because her father, the Marquess of Ailsa, had used St Margarets as his principal residence from 1817 until his death in 1846. Through him, she had many contacts with the gentry in Scotland, and through her husband and second son, she was familiar with all the entertainments beloved by those who devoted much of their leisure time to horse racing …'

In other grand houses of Twickenham, such as Cross Deep Hall, York House, Lebanon Park, Orleans House, North End House, Dial House, Pope's Villa and Strawberry Hill, wealthy owners and aristocrats led similar lives.

In 1892, a newly appointed district surveyor for Twickenham could see there would be pressure from increasing traffic and property development for an improved road between Twickenham and Richmond. Henry Little, now a county and Twickenham councillor, began to mediate in negotiations over the new road. Designs for York Street, a new road intended to route circulation away from the old Church Street, took on greater significance when Henry Foulkes acquired Cambridge House and Park in 1897, planning new houses, flats and shops that would bring in hundreds more residents. At the same time, Richmond Borough Council was campaigning to preserve the view from Richmond Hill, and any rich potential buyers of grand Twickenham property were beginning to move further out of London.

In 1898, the managing director of London United Tramways, J. Clifton Robinson, proposed to Twickenham Urban District Council to create the Hampton Loop, linking the main Hammersmith to Hampton Court line with a subsidiary line from the new York Street to Richmond Bridge. This was aimed to attract weekend day-trippers as well as facilitate the commute of 'working men' who were amongst the new residents. The subsidiary line was unable to progress beyond the bridge because of its narrow diameter and gradient.

Councillors with Middlesex County Council representing northern suburbs, however, wanted to make a deal with Metropolitan Tramway and Omnibus Company instead, and opposed the London United Tramways proposals. The County Council thus voted against it and petitioned the House of Lords, suggesting the clerks of Teddington and Twickenham councils had received 'improper payments' on signing agreements with Robinson's LUT.

A subsequent inquiry by the Light Railway Commissioners upheld the objections of the London & South Western Railway, claiming its own commercial interests were threatened. LUT was then forced to make use of a parliamentary Bill as a last resort.

Twickenham asked Middlesex County Council to withdraw any opposition to LUT, concerned about its powers under the Light Railways Act to purchase tramlines on county roads. A former county councillor and barrister, George James Duncan, led local opposition. Duncan had married the Richmond daughter of a celebrated medical writer and inventor of the respirator, Julius Jeffreys, and was living in East Twickenham. His petition to the House of Lords had seventy-four signatures, mainly from owners and tenants of large houses in Richmond Road and East Twickenham, concerned that 'the rural, pretty and residential character' of the area would suffer, and would 'deteriorate the value of the property enormously'. Other opponents included the Vicar of St Stephen's.

London United Tramways received the go-ahead via the special London United Tramways Act of 1900, and negotiations to widen the main roads of Twickenham, and use the new bypass (York Street) of old Twickenham village to reach Richmond Bridge, were completed in 1901.

Twickenham UDC (Urban District Council) was in part responding to property interests wanting to open up the area for development, but could not itself afford to fund the loans needed for investment. The LUT company was reinvigorated with a new board of directors and a new share issue.

Twickenham UDC had also signed a parallel agreement in October 1899 for the Twickenham and Teddington Electric Supply Company to construct the vital electricity grid in 1901–1902, which was duly inaugurated in July 1902 in time for the trams to open in 1903.

Richmond Bridge, from the East Twickenham side, c.1905. Gas lamps stand to attention at the bridge entrance; in the distance, the Talbot Hotel stands where the Odeon cinema is now.
(Postcard image provided by Alan Winter)

Richmond resisted being opened up by LUT, arguing that 'no existing thorough-fare will permit a line being constructed through the town', and favouring trams from Hammersmith Bridge or Putney instead.

Other issues prevented further transport development in the first decades of the twentieth century. Because London United Tramways was successful with its south-west London loops which finally terminated in East Twickenham, the Tube was never extended beyond Richmond. Discussions about trunk roads into London regularly delayed plans to widen Richmond Bridge: the carriageway was only 16 feet wide, so no tram system could go across it, and initially the only other option remained horse-drawn omnibuses. For a while, the local council had to focus on the future of the many grand houses by the Thames instead.

At the outbreak of World War I, East Twickenham tram services were still con-tinuing from Richmond Bridge. *Kelly's Directory for Middlesex* of 1914 listed:

> Electric Tram Cars pass through every three minutes from Shepherd's Bush & Hammersmith to Hampton Court; also Richmond Bridge to Teddington, King-ston & Tooting
> Motor omnibuses from Highgate, via Great Western station, Paddington, Westbourne Grove, Notting Hill, Hammersmith, Chiswick High road, Kew Gardens & Richmond, every 4 minutes
> Herne Hill & Teddington & Herne Hill & Hounslow motor omnibuses pass through Twickenham & St. Margaret's every 10 to 15 minutes
> Carriers to London.—London Parcels Delivery Co. Pick-fords Ltd. & Carter, Paterson & Co. Limited, daily

Tramway terminus at East Twickenham, 1906, showing uniformed staff alongside and a single track in the road (Postcard image provided by Kenneth Lea)

Richmond Road looking towards the bridge, corner of Morley Road (Photo by kind permission of David King)

Motorised buses arrived locally in 1910, with 'Twickenham Garage' used as a bus depot. Built in 1912 on the site of the earlier proposed roller-skating rink, next door to Cambridge House and perpendicular from Cambridge Road with an exit in the parallel Clevedon Road, it remained in operation until 1971. An unconfirmed report says that it was requisitioned by the Royal Flying Corps in WWI, reopening as a bus garage in 1919. During the early 1920s, it was used as a workshop for building and repairing bodywork on buses. The destination on buses for return journeys to the depot referred to this location as Richmond Bridge.

The trams only survived on this route until the 1920s. LUT plans to convert the East Twickenham route to the trolleybus were opposed by both Twickenham Council and Middlesex County Council on the grounds that Cambridge and Clevedon Roads were unsuitable for the proposed turning loop. (A trolleybus used rubber road tyres and was powered by overhead electricity cables, but needed a turning loop, unlike a bi-directional tram.) Twickenham Highways Committee then proposed that Cambridge Park, Morley and Alexandra Roads would be more suitable, but this too was opposed by residents. LUT thus renounced their plans and resolved to close the route and allow the General (London General Omnibus Company) to run a 'motorbus' service instead.

As Geoffrey Wilson wrote in his history of London United Tramways:

1930s photograph of a No. 27 bus at the bus stop between Cambridge and Cresswell Roads (Photo provided by Kenneth Lea)

> 'The Richmond Bridge – Twickenham section closed on October 1, 1924. The Richmond & Twickenham Times of October 4th had an editorial "The Last Voyage (by our own Tram Mariner)". It ran : "We put to sea from the harbour at Twickenham – whew ! it was a rough night ! – under the skilful guidance of Driver S. Cook, who has been with the old vessels for many years, and was accompanied by that sturdy helmsman Conductor Wright, who had proved himself, man and boy, a right good conductor, since the ships of the road first put to sea . . . There were few aboard. They included two lovers, a medley of raindrop dodgers and the reporter. It seemed as if the wraith of Sir Clifton Robinson was standing in the door-way of this, the last tram, and reminding us that the company had since its inception earned the gratitude of the travelling public, especially for the courtesy of their servants, on the very heavily used Hampton Court lines.'

The writer wound up this not unkindly notice by saying that there was reason for congratulation that the service was not otherwise to be curtailed and th[at] the board was still devising better, quicker and cheaper travel.'

This in turn opened up East Twickenham to better 'bus' connections with Richmond in the future. In 1932 to 1933 the London Transport Passenger Board took over all the remaining LUT routes. In 1994, when the bus services were privatised, the new company became London United Transport, echoing the former Tramways company name. Subsequent mergers and acquisitions renamed it Transdev and finally as London United.

On closure of the Cambridge Road garage in 1971, all of its routes and vehicles were transferred to Fulwell bus garage, but the building continued to be owned by London Transport until the mid-1990s.

The Museum of London Archaeology Service evaluated the garage site in 1983. Apart from identifying 'post-medieval' (nineteenth-century) reclamation dumps in their eastern trench, they commented retrospectively: 'The susceptibility of the area to flooding, while disadvantageous to settled agricultural communities, could be exploited for hunting and fowling by hunting groups. The gently sloping bank would facilitate the manhandling of boats into the River for fishing. This presumably influenced the site of the Richmond Ferry in later periods.'

The garage was used for the storage of privately owned old London Transport buses for the Routemaster Heritage Trust. The Trust was set up to provide secure accommodation for the restoration and preservation of old Routemasters and other buses once they became surplus to requirements. On 17 October 1992, the Cambridge Road garage was reopened by the Trust, which subsequently held open days for the public.

London Transport finally sold the Twickenham building for redevelopment and the Trust moved in late May 1994 to the former Norbiton garage for eight months, which was also slated for demolition. The Trust was later renamed the Classic Bus Heritage Trust. Modern town houses now stand on the Twickenham site where buses once rested between shifts.

The Routemaster Heritage Trust base in Cambridge Road, during an open day in 1993, with a fine line of Routemaster buses. Far right is an ex-London Transport bus, with a early green bus behind. (Photo by Clive Warneford/ Twickenham Bus Garage/ CC BY-SA 2.0 licence)

With regard to private ownership of transport, the tram service arrived on the streets in 1903 just as horse-drawn conveyances were beginning to be replaced by motorised vehicles. To support these, garage services started to appear in Richmond Road and its offshoots – some remain a century later, such as Kwikfit, and the MOT centre in the former Gaiety Cinema.

A plot of land in the corner of Denton and Morley Roads was sold in 1907 to Sir Henry Evan Murchison James, the owner of Glenshee in Cambridge Park, which lay to the rear. Sir Henry had progressed from carriage and horse to the newly invented motor car, and built a garage on the new land with space for three cars, and chauffeur's quarters above. This garage was known as Barrock Park, 62 Morley Road, and exists today, now converted to three houses.

One older resident of Morley Road remembers there being only one car originally in the street, a Daimler, which was available to hire for special occasions: in the 1960s this grew to three cars. Today, it is often challenging to find a parking space in local roads, despite the borough introducing residents' parking restrictions in the 1990s. Even for city-bound Londoners, the convenience of personal cars quickly caught on.

In 2020, Richmond Borough introduced a 20mph speed limit over many of its streets – other 'green' policies have perhaps been more universally welcomed. Lower council charges for hybrid or electric cars have increased their popularity, with such vehicles ever more apparent as residents stretch cables and protectors over the pavement; these are now being replaced by charging points in the base of street lamps, indicated by a blue LED light.

Technological advances have come and gone over the last one hundred and twenty years. Today, changes accelerated by the 2020–21 Covid-19 crisis may produce lasting benefits in how the population owns and fuels cars, travels and uses public transport, much as the crisis of World War II, some eighty years earlier resulted in significant social and economic transformation across the UK. Those wartime disruptions to daily life affected not only transport but every aspect of human existence, and on a scale never seen before or since.

Barrock Park, 62 Morley Road, in the early 20th century, from the sale notice for Glenshee in Cambridge Park (Richmond upon Thames Local Studies Library and Archive)

Left: The three 'new' houses converted from the garage on the corner of Denton and Morley Roads, 2020. (Photo by Jonathan Crofts)

CHAPTER 22
LIFE UNDER ATTACK

Preparations in the Twickenham area for the Second World War were much the same as for the rest of London. Responsibilities for protecting the population were delegated to local authorities, and started as early as November 1936 with uncertainty over the worsening political situation. Volunteers joined as ARP (Air Raid Precautions) wardens, in the Home Guard, or as rescue and demolition workers or fire-watchers, while others remained in 'reserved occupations' for war work.

Protecting the public from invasion began in earnest after the Munich Agreement of 1938, and millions of sandbags to protect buildings were ordered, along with gas masks and medical supplies. By January 1939, these preparations had to be accelerated, as a shortage of air-raid wardens, trench-diggers and first-aid posts was identified in the borough. The Twickenham Communists proposed deep underground shelters for the whole population, but this was rejected as too costly.

Wartime activities included avoiding waste, 'digging for Victory', and of course coping with food rationing: meat, bacon, ham, sugar, butter, margarine and cooking fats were the first to be limited. Fund-raising weeks were arranged, and gas masks were issued to everyone (although as the war went on, many people stopped carrying them). In the middle of August 1939, Richmond, Twickenham and the surrounding areas rehearsed a full-scale blackout.

One effect of wartime government intervention was the requisitioning of the iron gates and railings in front of houses in local roads. Edwardian and Victorian houses throughout London and the rest of the country surrendered their metal, losing some of their elegance in the process. Only then was it discovered that the metal could not be used for war purposes, being of the wrong type. In later years, the front garden of many properties were lost altogether, of course, in favour of parking considerations. In their heyday, Morley Road and its neighbours were once regarded as so uniformly stylish that people would visit in order to admire them and take photographs, in an age when cameras were not the everyday items they are now.

War was finally declared on 3 September 1939, and the *Richmond & Twickenham Times* reported:

> 'With a quiet, dignified loyalty Twickenham responded to the call which came on Sunday morning, when the Prime Minister told a troubled world that at last this country had been compelled to declare war on Germany. The suspense of the last few weeks gave place to a feeling almost of relief ...'

That initial relief quickly evolved into a waiting game over the first eight months, later dubbed as the 'Phoney War'. After trying to destroy the Royal Air Force over the Channel and South East England from June 1940, Hitler then ordered night-time attacks on London. The first bombing in the Twickenham area began in August. Civilians protected themselves in Anderson shelters (portable steel frames covered with earth for extra protection), sometimes spending the night in them, or in Morrison shelters, similar to a caged steel table which people would sit or sleep under. Another option were the public shelters that had been constructed across the borough: there was one in Marble Hill Park, with capacity for three hundred and fifty-five people, located near the entrance to the park opposite the Rising Sun

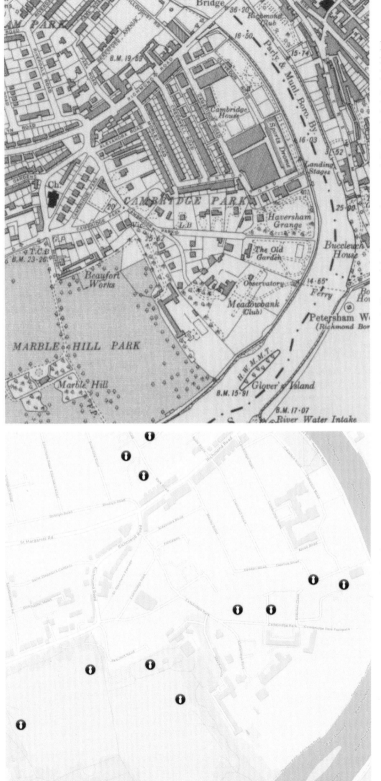

pub. The Twickenham ARP map shows further public shelters on the junction of Richmond Road with Morley Road, and by Richmond Bridge. The Morley Road shelter lay just behind the dairy on the corner: when that property recently came up for sale, the marketing photos suggested an unusual amount of basement space.

Early on during this Luftwaffe 'Blitzkrieg' ('lightning war' in German), a 2,000 lb bomb landed on the Richmond Ice Rink (still formally known as the Sports-Drome). Instead of exploding, it slid along the ice into the machinery room, and a bomb disposal team were able to remove it. The rink reopened the following day to the delight of all.

Nonetheless, the bus garage and adjoining houses in Cambridge and Clevedon Roads were badly hit in October 1940.

Top: Ordnance Survey map of 1939 (revised 1934–1935). The Beaufort Works, bombed in 1940, is visible on the north side of Marble Hill Park (Reproduced with the permission of the National Library of Scotland)

Left: High-explosive bombs dropped during the London Blitz, 7 October 1940 to 6 June 1941 (Image with kind permission of the National Archives, www.bombsight.org)

The cause of it
30th Sept 1940.
SPORTS - DROME
E. Twickenham
nr Richmond Bridge

Richmond Ice Rink
suffered
a 2000 lb bomb
- fortunately
it did not
explode!

2

Above: The 2,000 lb bomb which landed on the Richmond Ice Rink and slid into the machinery room where a bomb disposal team removed it.

Right: Bus garage showing ambulances and vehicles prior to bomb damage

Air raid damage at Twickenham bus garage, Clevedon Road, shown in the *Topical Press*, 24 Oct 1940. After clearing debris, repair work began with stripping away the wrecked sections of the roof. The neighbouring houses beyond also suffered considerable damage. Rubble and debris ring the bomb crater on the forecourt, below.
(Photos © TfL from the London Transport Museum Collection)

The heaviest toll was seventy-four people killed on the night of 29 November 1940, although the worst damage was in the Teddington area, near the National Physics Laboratory (where Sir Barnes Wallis did early work on the famous bouncing bomb used in the devastating 1943 'Dambusters' raid). In East Twickenham, there was considerable damage to the Beaufort Engineering Works on the north edge of Marble Hill Park, by what is now the car park.

All hands to deck after the bomb attack on the Beaufort Works – home of AMD Engineering (see Chapter 18).
Reg Vine was the milk boy, in the cap, bottom right (Photo by permission of Keith Barrett Photographer: Frank Dann)

Martyn Day of the St Margarets Community Website (www.stmargarets.london) paints a vivid picture of the November 1940 attack: 'The Nazi bombers came at night from the east, navigating their way along the Thames to their aiming points in South West London. We will probably never know what the Luftwaffe crews were actually aiming at but on Friday 29th November 1940, in a raid that lasted nearly 6½ hours, some 130 high explosive bombs and between 3,000 and 5,000 incendiary devices rained down on St Margarets, Twickenham, Richmond, Isleworth and Teddington, destroying 150 houses and damaging more than 6,000

Reg Vine was a local milk boy, living in Morley Road at the time. He went to Orleans School and had worked at Jarvis Stores, the grocers, and then at Hornby & Clarke (later Express Dairies), on the corner of Morley Road:

'We were standing outside the shop the night they had the great air raid on Richmond. It was the night Richmond caught fire – it was a right old night. I'd lived in a house opposite the factory before the war … at the age of fifteen, I went to Dunkirk with the Twickenham Sea Cadets.

The AMD factory was rebuilt on the same site and after serving in the Royal Navy, I worked for them for some years, producing aircraft parts. This is now the site of a modern row of mews houses.'

Twickenham Sea Cadets' first Commanding Officer, Lt Willing, led a number of the cadets as part of the Dunkirk evacuation. Taking the unit's motor launch *Rummy II*, they came under fire and saved 140 servicemen. Lt Willing was awarded the Distinguished Service Cross and the unit was renamed 'TS Willing' in his honour.

Reg Vine also featured more recently in Sinclair McKay's book *Dunkirk: From Disaster to Deliverance – Testimonies of the Last Survivors* (2015, Aurum Press Ltd). His later wartime experience was on Royal Navy aircraft carriers in the Mediterranean, the Far East and the Arctic.

Following the war, Reg went on to work as an actor and male model, in TV adverts, BBC plays and advertising posters and stills: the highest profile was on The Who's 1973 vinyl record sleeve for their album *Quadrophenia*. In the 1970s he also worked as a Special Constable for the Thames River Police.

Reg was part of the Vine Chimney Sweep family, a local business established in 1850, and the current owner is the fifth generation of sweeps in the family.

others. It was the area's biggest raid of the 2nd World War. A German government communique stated later that it was a "Reprisal Raid" directed towards military targets.

There were many casualties. Mr and Mrs Sydney Clark and their dog were killed by the sheer concussion of a large bomb 5 feet high and 18 inches wide that crashed into their dining room. The bomb failed to explode. Mrs Dawson and her 2 children died under falling masonry. Tom Brown, an old soldier and his wife, were both blown up. They had known each other since childhood. One bomb hit an underground shelter causing the deaths of 8 wives and children of men all disabled in the 1st World War. Another bomb hit a pub and killed 16 customers … The list goes on and on.

Because of their own self-imposed censorship the local newspapers reported the raid in generalities. The *Thames Valley Times* is typical. In its issue of 4 December 1940 it reported that "2 hospitals were damaged, a Baptist church was gutted, cinemas were hit and a municipal building fell under the rain of incendiary bombs". That municipal building was Richmond Town Hall. The caretaker living on the premises first put out an incendiary in his own bedroom, then opened the door to find the entire roof of the building missing, the central staircase exposed to the sky and the Town Hall surrounded by flames twenty to thirty feet high. When they came to clear up the mess afterwards they found melted coins, silver cups and the Town Crier's bell buried in the rubble.

There were many hundreds of fires. One fire station reported over 164 alone. The most spectacular was Beaumont Furniture Works in Beaumont Road, St Margarets. It was packed with soft furnishings and furniture and it went up like a firework. Mr Maugham, the manager, managed to rescue 3 horses and some domestic rabbits from the blazing stables. Then with the help of the fire services and local neighbours he was able to get the fire under control. When Mr. Maugham eventually got home he found his own bedroom on fire. One local woman found an incendiary blazing away merrily on top of her hallstand. She extinguished the fire by emptying an ancient aspidistra on top of it – the same plant that she had only agreed to keep after her husband pleaded for its life a few days earlier.

An incendiary fell into the Circle of a Richmond cinema. Their own fire team put it out so quickly that the film was hardly interrupted. The manager announced the danger was over, the audience cheered and settled back to enjoy the rest of the film. Then another incendiary fell into the Stalls. As the seats blazed and the cinema's own coke store caught fire the audience was calmly led to safety.

One family took shelter from falling masonry under their kitchen table along with the family dog. When it was over the 6-year-old daughter, still trapped in the rubble, said "When I get out of this I will write that Hitler such a dirty letter!" A Public Library caught alight as well. The sign over the door, "Books make black-outs brighter", proving only too true.

When it was all over and the outcome of the raid being considered, the *Richmond & Twickenham Times* (7 December 1940) urged its readers to ignore exaggerated reports about the number of casualties … "accept our word for the fact that casualties in the London area are very light in view of the damage done."

The same "chin-up" mood was echoed in the *Richmond Herald* of the same date: "The bombed out towns come up smiling!", it reported. "High explosive and incendiary bombs rained down with indiscriminating ferocity. The air was heavy with the odour of charred timber. Firemen's hoses lay along the gutter and jets of water were being played upon smouldering debris – but the traffic was unimpeded and the business life in the district proceeded normally."

None of this bothered Mr Rodgers, a 55 year old caretaker arrested in Richmond the day after the raid, drunk and incapable. He claimed that he was returning to his work at Lion House to check the boiler. In court the magistrate pointed out that it was not the wisest thing to be attending to a boiler in a drunken state. Mr Rodgers, now sober and contrite, said that he wasn't actually intending to work on the boiler – he was only going to the boiler house to sleep!'

During the 1940 to 1941 Blitz, Denton Road suffered a total of two bombs, and Cambridge Park (including where Roseleigh Close is now sited) similarly. There were three recorded in Marble Hill Park, and three more on the north side of Richmond Road.

On the afternoon of 31 January 1941, incendiaries were dropped around St Stephen's Church, one of them falling through the roof and exploding in a pew. Mr Bray, the verger, rapidly extinguished it, and was later congratulated by one of his congregation:

> 'Saint Stephen's Church shall be my prey!
> Within God's House my flames I'll play!
> Thus Satan spake; but Verger Bray
> With Christian zeal, quenched Hell that day.'

From June 1941, attacks on London reduced as the German Luftwaffe focussed their efforts on Russia and the Eastern Front, with only one raid reaching Twickenham between 1942 and 1943. On 20 April 1943, a single twin-engined aircraft approached the borough from the east on its way to Slough. In perfect conditions, with full moon, no cloud and no wind, a 500 kg high explosive bomb missed houses directly, but fell on a footpath just to the east of Cambridge Park: it destroyed 30 feet of brick wall, a 3-inch water main, and broke glass in thirty houses nearby.

The Cambridge Park area was lucky to escape conventional bombing in the 'Little Blitz' of early 1944, although other parts of Twickenham Borough suffered. From June of that year, however, London was menaced by V1 rockets – unmanned and unpredictable in their aim, the buzz of the pulsejet engine would suddenly cut out, leaving the rocket to glide silently to earth. In the 1940 raids, people had at least heard the bombs whistle on their way down, offering some level of warning. Each rocket carried 849 kg of high explosive. Twickenham as a whole suffered from twenty-seven such landings. The last fatality in the district took place on 29 August.

The Cambridge Park area was not left unmarked. On 5 July 1944, a 'doodlebug' or 'buzz bomb', as they were known, fell on Teddington Studios, at that time the film studios of the Warner Brothers. Some two thousand gallons of diesel oil were scattered and ignited. The film currently in production, *Flight from Folly*, was finished off in a garage, but the studios were forced to close by October. Eric Bourne was then film correspondent of the *Richmond & Twickenham Times* and lost a friend there in the attack. He later recalled: '… for days after the bombing a multitude of dead fish collected near Richmond Bridge. They had been poisoned by the oil which flowed down the Thames.'

By July 1944, as a result of these attacks, Twickenham Borough saw the evacuation of seven thousand more women and children. Fortunately, the later and even more terrifying V2 rockets could barely reach Twickenham from their missile bases – only one fell on the borough, with no fatalities.

Personal accounts demonstrate the long-term damage caused by the bombing. In *War Widows Stories*, produced by the eponymous organisation celebrating and commemorating the lives and sacrifices of those who have fought and fallen in service for their country (www.warwidowsstories.org.uk), Jeannie Benjamin recounts the story of her mother Margaret Benjamin who was widowed when her husband Eric Benjamin (Jeannie's father) was killed in action during the Second World War. Margaret was left with two young daughters, Jeannie, aged eighteen months, and Sally, just three weeks old. Some years later, the family was offered a council flat in the old Haversham Grange: 'I grew up originally in a pre-fab in Hounslow. We moved there from my grandmother's house after my father was killed [in the war]. So we lived there until I was about five or six, and then we moved to a council flat in east Twickenham, which was a big, old, rambling house called Haversham Grange, which was divided into flats. I had a great childhood. I had a huge, huge garden which led into a wood near the river Thames, and we used to go and camp in there and play out. There was an old bombed house in one corner and we went … It was very dangerous, but we had a great time. And that was a nice childhood.'

CHAPTER 23
POST-WAR LIVING

Overall, Twickenham came off relatively lightly from the Second World War compared to other parts of London. Nonetheless, there were bombed-out, homeless people to house, and returning servicemen and women to provide with occupations and in some cases accommodation.

Cambridge House had been demolished in 1937, although the bus garage and Sports-Drome (the Ice Rink) remained, together with Richmond Bridge Works.

Flooding continued to cause problems in the neighbourhood until central government came up with a London-wide solution in the 1980s. The pre-war damage caused by the worst widespread flooding of 1928 is still remembered locally, as described by Martyn Day: 'Aidan Clarke, a columnist with the *Richmond & Twickenham Times*, didn't get much sleep …

Ordnance Survey map of 1960 showing a large car park next to the Richmond Bridge Works in Cambridge Road, opposite the tennis courts (still present in 2021) and its former public lavatories (since demolished) (Reproduced with the permission of the National Library of Scotland)

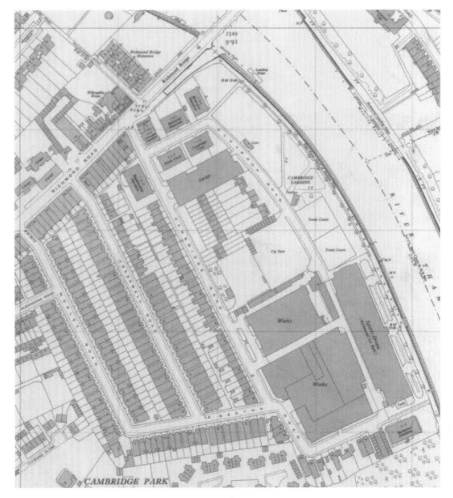

"I heard no bells when New Year 1928 came in, except the striking of the clock. I don't say that there were no bells, but their sound did not reach me … When I opened the door (according to my invariable custom) at a minute before midnight; lifeless, rawly cold, the thaw proceeding; drip, drip, drip, most melancholy… silence, plus the drippity, drip, drip, drip of the melting snows of yester-year."

Heavy snow had fallen over the Christmas holiday followed by a sudden thaw on New Year's Eve and then unusually heavy rain. The amount of water coming down the Thames doubled, coinciding with a high spring tide and a storm surge coming up the river. Water levels in the Thames Estuary rose to 4 feet above normal. Further upstream as the river narrowed water levels rose even more. At 1.30am on the morning of Saturday 7 January 1928 the river reached 18'3' above the datum line – the highest water level ever recorded. At Teddington Lock water was pouring over the weir at nine thousand million gallons every twenty-four hours. From Greenwich to Twickenham and up the tidal reaches of the River Crane, the embankments holding the torrent began to fail. By around 2am, flood water was pouring into St Margarets, Richmond and East Twickenham.

Later that same day, the *Richmond & Twickenham Times* took up the story:

"Residents roused at 2.00am! The highest tide in living memory came up into the roadway, invaded the shops on the Twickenham side of Richmond Bridge and held up car traffic and pedestrians. From midnight until four o'clock the roadway was under water to a depth of over a foot … All the ground floors of the flats were flooded and for over 200 yards along the Richmond Road water was level with the shops' ground floors."'

Following a visit to the affected area with the Revd H Martyn Sanders, vicar of St Stephen's, the Mayor of Twickenham, Councillor William C Robinson, testified that: "It is in East Twickenham that the loss is greatest. Along Park Road and the neighbourhood of Richmond Bridge most basements are flooded out and practically everything in them spoiled. In some cases people were sleeping below and they narrowly escaped with their lives."

Martyn Day continues: 'The *Richmond Herald* also had the following report tucked away in a corner. Lord Desborough, chairman of the Thames Conservancy Board, stated at a meeting on Monday,

"What happened the other day was that a high tide, amounting almost to a bore, came up the North Sea. That is the cause, and not altogether the Thames water. Not even the Thames Conservancy, nor the Port of London Authority, can stop the water coming in from the North Sea. The only way I can see is the one that was suggested, and which I recommended 21 years ago. That is, to put a barrage from Tilbury to Gravesend, with locks in it."'

Prior to approval of the Thames Barrier, the then MP for Twickenham, Toby Jessel, spoke in 1972 before Parliament of the flood prevention measures required locally: 'In East Twickenham, in my constituency, the GLC two years ago built flood walls as an interim emergency measure to save a considerable number of local residents who live on low-lying ground nearby, some in basements, from the risk of being drowned and also to prevent damage to houses in the area.

The cost of that work was only £60,000, which in my view was abundantly justified even if the work is required for only about eight years, until the main barrier is built.

… The risk of such a surge coming up the Thames is increasing every year because London is sinking relative to the level of the sea and also because of the channels that are made in the Thames Estuary by dredgers facilitating supertankers coming up the estuary, helping surges to flow upstream. It is absolutely right that the Bill should go ahead at full speed.'

Lord Desborough's words back in 1928 were prophetic, although it was fifty-six years before the Thames Barrier was finally opened in 1984.

Residential building development alongside the capricious Thames was nonetheless to continue after WWII. Richmond Local Studies noted in 2009:

'A speculative building firm (St Alban's Investments Ltd.) put forward, in 1958, a plan to build a series of lock-up garages in the Haversham Grange grounds in Cambridge Park, East Twickenham and applied for the modification of the restrictive covenants to enable them to carry out this work. The application was opposed by both the Richmond and Twickenham Borough Councils, together with other local authorities and private individuals. The case went before the Lands Tribunal who decided not to revoke the covenants and the firm was ordered to pay the agreed costs of each objector who was legally represented.'

Even so, between 1958 and 1974, Jeremiah Little's design for Cambridge Park was transformed, and not to universal acclaim. Developers such as True Bond Homes and Sterling Homes knocked down all the houses on the north side of Cambridge Park from Haversham Grange to Alexandra Road, saving only Nos. 36 and 40. More were demolished and huge trees felled to make room for new roads, two named after the houses they replaced – Haversham Close and Beaulieu Close. Next followed Roseleigh Close, Vivienne Close, Fairlawns and Powers Court. Thirteen Victorian villas were replaced by one hundred and forty-two houses and maisonettes and three blocks of flats. At Beaconsfield, No. 36, a house was built on each of the once generous side lawns.

Beaconsfield, 36 Cambridge Park, from the auction catalogue, 1910 (left) and in 2020 (right) (Photo by Jonathan Crofts)

Cambridge Park Mews, behind Alexandra and Morley Roads, had degenerated into slums by the 1960s and were demolished at the same time as the Archdeacon Cambridge's charmingly rustic entrance lodge on the corner of Alexandra Road, which was replaced by a small block of flats of the same name, Ely Lodge, named after Archdeacon Cambridge's position as a Prebendary of Ely Cathedral. Some rebuilding took place in Henry Foulkes' Denton Road as a result of bomb damage incurred during the Second World War, with further demolition and rebuilding later in 2020-21.

Richmond Road continued to evolve. It even had more than one bank – the Midland Bank on the corner of Cresswell Road and the Westminster Bank on the corner of Rosslyn Road, both now occupied by dental services. For some years, there were three garages – one on the site of the modern-day Kwikfit, and an Esso station opposite the end of Morley Road, plus the MOT garage at the back of the old cinema building.

Twickenham resident Dave Hall looks back with affection on the early 1960s in Richmond Road: 'As a 16 year old I started work back in 1960 at the old Westminster Bank at 351 Richmond Road, East Twickenham. I was there for about 6 years until I was transferred to another branch. As for that part of the road leading to the bridge … I remember … the shops and businesses at that time. Sanders Garage was near the bank and was owned by a Mr Cheshire.

The Esso garage, formerly the Grand Garage, on Richmond Road, c.1965, next to the former Gaiety Cinema and billiards hall, with the Tony Lane betting shop in the left-hand shop front (Twickenham Park Residents Association)

The *Richmond & Twickenham Times* reported the Mayor of Richmond's purchase of an Austin York saloon car from the Grand Garage in Richmond Road in the 1930s (Richmond upon Thames Local Studies Library and Archive)

An air pump, c.1973, on the old forecourt of the Grand Garage – the car repair business and petrol station that once existed in front of 'old' Ryde House in Richmond Road, facing Morley Road. The office was in Ryde House. Note the Express Dairy opposite. (Photo by Tony McSweeney)

This is now a Kwik Fit. There was a cobbler's and I believe that is still there. There was a newsagent's which was run by a family called Morey. The manager when I joined the bank was a Mr Sice and he and his family lived above the branch. Later on there were solicitors who moved into the premises, Herbert Baron & Co. On the next corner a gentleman named Xenaphon Georgiades opened a cafe … These premises are now the Orpheus Taverna. Further along there was Grand Garages which was on a substantial site, now gone and redeveloped. I used to go to Gino's for my haircut, this was back in the days when I had hair! Ah memories. On the other side of the road there was Midland Bank, Cresswell Cafe and a fish and chip shop. Just around the corner there was a post office.'

Fellow resident Martin Levey picks up the memory trail: '… opposite the Nat West – Abrahams the tailors, Lett Bros (estate agents), Ensors the typewriter shop. Forests the grocer's, Swaynes the greengrocer's, the Wool Shop and Fairing Shop! Another shoe repair shop, the Post Office, Hairdresser's, dry cleaner's and a newsagent's on the corner of Alexandra Road… Next to Charles Harry the chemist, there was a cycle shop, launderette, tailor's, fruit and veg shop (Bush), then Mr Pope the grocer and on the corner of Morley Road, Hornby and Clarke, dairy. On the other corner, Co-op butcher, then Co-op grocer and next to that Rawlings, furniture shop…'

At No. 393 Richmond Road is 'old' Ryde House, a small Italianate stucco villa, with a golden hawk over the door. Ryde House was originally built in 1832, it is rumoured, for the operator of the first Richmond to Hyde Park Corner horse-drawn bus service. One local older resident remembers it as the home of a local doctor in the 1960s. It was restored in the 1980s by the Thomas Saunders Partnership as part of the adjacent development of No. 397 into offices for a building society, plus twenty-four flats and two shops. The London Goldhawk Building Society – hence the gilded bird of prey – relocated from Chiswick, and the redeveloped Ryde House opened in March 1979, restored at a cost of approximately £100k. Prince Charles' Duchy Originals brand subsequently moved here in 2004.

The Richmond Corner House in the 1960s at 369 Richmond Road, now the Orpheus Taverna (Howard Webb Collection)

David King, a local resident who grew up in Richmond Bridge Mansions, recalls that the legacy of Henry Foulkes, the builder and developer of this part of East Twickenham, was not just restricted to his building of the new 'suburb' at the turn of the twentieth century: his granddaughter Daphne helped run the bar of the Mary Wallace Theatre in Twickenham during the 1990s.

The earlier grand mansions of the London wealthy have been replaced by Foulkes' suburban houses, shops, and flats in mansion blocks, which have for the most part survived two world wars and other national crises. But despite these large-scale developments, the local tradition of building grand houses was not to disappear completely.

Ryde House, 393 Richmond Road, under redevelopment in 1978 (Richmond upon Thames Local Studies Library and Archive)

Ryde House, Richmond Road,
after restoration
(Richmond upon Thames
Local Studies Library
and Archive)

CHAPTER 24
THE NEW OLD GARDEN

Over the Thames from the site known as The Old Garden, where Henry Little's Cambridge Park House once stood, slopes lead down to the public promenade along Richmond riverside. These grounds once formed part of a large private estate owned by the 4th Earl of Cardigan, and subsequently inherited in 1790 by his daughter, Elizabeth, Duchess of Buccleuch. It was here in 1842 that the 5th Duke of Buccleuch, Elizabeth's grandson, entertained Queen Victoria and Prince Albert. The Buccleuch pleasure gardens were then extended right across the river by Sir John Whittaker Ellis, who had acquired the property on the opposite bank in 1896, including The Old Garden.

From 1902, this verdant space lay within the purview of the Richmond, Petersham and Ham Open Spaces Act, created to preserve the fine vista from Richmond Hill, for so long the inspiration for writers and artists.

Later in the twentieth century, The Old Garden was acquired by Peter Mead, co-founder in 1977 of Abbott Mead Vickers, which grew into one of the advertising industry's most respected and highly awarded agencies, AMV BBDO. In 1995, it became the largest advertising agency in the UK, has won numerous 'Agency of the Year' awards, and was chosen in 2015 by the Sunday Times as one of Britain's best employers.

Mead's career included many board appointments, including at Wembley National Stadium and with the London Docklands Development Corporation. He served as the vice-chairman of the NSPCC Full Stop Appeal, chairman of Omnicom Europe and vice-chairman of Omnicom Group Inc.

He was awarded a CBE in 2013 for services to the Creative Industries. In 2014, his book of anecdotes and observations on life and his career, *When In Doubt Be Nice: Lessons From a Lifetime In Business*, was published by Silvertail Books.

Peter Mead grew up in Peckham, where his father owned a window-cleaning business. His spectacular career in advertising began at the age of sixteen when he joined the despatch department of a large agency, straight out of school.

Having been a loyal Millwall supporter since childhood, Mead bought into the football club and became vice-chairman, then chairman.

'I thought I could improve things in Abbott Mead-style by some open, friendly ideas,' he said. 'Well, I now have the unenviable record of being the only football club chairman who was top of the division in December and relegated in the following May.'

The club eventually went into liquidation, with Mead reputed to have lost £3m in the process. His son Billy was in the Millwall team for a while too. In a *Management Today* interview of September 2000, Peter Mead was quoted as saying:

'The main problem was that, as a boss, you were completely removed from what happened on the pitch ... It's bloody hard to influence that. It's a brutal business, where people get used to being abused ... I tell you, if you think institutions and the City are impatient masters, try facing football fans in the car park.'

After this experience Mead agreed to become patron of the Andrea Adams Trust, an anti-bullying charity. In the same interview in 2000, he said:

'Philip Larkin [the poet] said: 'Life is a beginning, a muddle and an end.' I don't think work should contribute disproportionately to that muddle.'

Peter Mead was often identified in his industry as the 'nice guy'. In a *Monocle* interview of April 2015, he was quoted again:

'At the core of everything I believe about business is the word "relationships" ... Developing relationships – if you spend all your life doing that you won't go far wrong.'

RTT 12.6.1981

The Old Garden
(*Richmond and
Twickenham Times*,
12 June 1981)

LOOKING as though it should be in a Hollywood film, this house, set in three acres of landscaped grounds at Cambridge Park, East Twickenham, is on the market for a spectacular £600,000.

The owner, who does not want his name dis-closed, is the chairman of a well-known London football club.

Both the house and grounds have all the trappings of wealth. Inside is a billiards - entertainments room with a raised entertainment area. There are three other reception rooms, a luxurious fitted kitchen, four bedroom suites with bathrooms, and a two-roomed, self-contained flat.

Outside, the grounds are landscaped with a central path lined with pollarded lime trees. There is an ornamental lily pond, and a rose garden with central fish pond and a fountain.

There is also a hard tennis court and a heated swimming pool — and 350ft. river frontage.

Agents handling the property are Savills, of Mount Street, W1.

Buccleuch House on the Richmond side, later demolished in 1938, was sold by Sir John Whittaker Ellis, together with the pleasure grounds and conservatory on the Middlesex bank in 1902. Early in the 1920s, a large house was erected among the old lawns and shrubberies, following the popular mock-Tudor style of the period, and strictly observing the building line covenanted in 1861 between John Parson and George Bishop.

This house, named 'The Old Garden', was architect-designed and merited five full pages of photographs in *The Ideal Home* magazine of June 1926. Initially the gardens remained in their original design. Between 1934 and 1936, however, the large conservatory was taken down and replaced by a block of flats known as Cambridge Park Court, which remain today.

The Old Garden site enabled the tradition of building grand houses on the banks of the Thames to continue into the second decade of the twenty-first century. Sitting in more than three acres of grounds with ancient trees, hedgerows and manicured lawns, The (New) Old Garden is an imposing Palladian-style mansion within easy walking distance of Richmond.

The four-floor building, designed by the renowned architect Quinlan Terry CBE, architect equally of the Richmond Riverside development by the bridge, is approached through solid oak entrance gates, with a short carriage drive leading into the forecourt at the front of the house.

According to the property particulars in 2014, hidden behind these oak gates The Old Garden opens into a grand reception hall, with features inspired by The Great Hall in Oxfordshire (presumed to be Ditchley Park, as used in the 2009 film *The Young Victoria*) and an ancient carving from Rome. On the ground floor, the property also has more than a dozen rooms, including a steam room, gymnasium, indoor swimming pool and staff quarters. The eight main bedrooms of the house are located on the first and second floors. The master suite takes up one end of the first floor and includes his-and-her bathrooms and dressing rooms.

The (New) Old Garden, built in 2014 by the architect Quinlan Terry. (Photo by James Brittain)

On the lower ground floor are a snooker or games room, a cinema and numerous storerooms. There is a garage with space for three cars, and 'room for a further three if a car stacker is installed'. The front courtyard can accommodate up to twenty vehicles.

The 2014 property description emphasised the target market for the house: '… if the new owner would rather fly in, there is ample room in the grounds for a helicopter landing spot, too, subject to the necessary consents. Being on the eastern point of a long, lazy loop of the Thames between Richmond Bridge and Eel Pie Island, there is also the potential to install a mooring on the water. The grounds include a tennis court and a swimming pool in addition to large open spaces, a pond, yew hedgerows and a herbaceous border.'

The list included the potential for a campshed mooring – a jetty projecting from the shore in the form of a long wooden or iron box filled with gravel, stones and mud.

Quinlan Terry wrote of the house in the property particulars: 'Classical residential architecture more than any other art form is dependent on the opportunities an architect is given. The Old Garden is one such case, as it is rare to find such a beautiful site on the banks of the Thames so close to London. The situation reminds me of my architectural hero, Palladio, who designed many beautiful villas along the banks of the Brenta in Italy.

'Historically, West London has always been the place for grand villas and many classical houses were built in the area during the 18th and 19th centuries. These distinguished neighbours were always in my mind, from the time I started drawing out the first scheme to completing the details. I also have personal affection for the area as I designed Richmond Riverside only half a mile away on the other side of the Thames, which was the first major commission of my career.

'However, this project differs from all of my other work, because I could pursue my interpretation of classicism with the purity and rigour that this circumstance allowed. I always think that the highest praise an architect can receive is to be told that the finished work looks as if it has always been there. With such buildings as Marble Hill, Petersham Lodge and Asgill House nearby, I hope this will be the reaction of those who see and visit the completed building.'

Garden design and landscaping was by Randle Siddeley, a 'leading landscape architecture and urban design practice in London', established over forty years previously. Their experience includes 'master-planning, landscaping and public realm designs in some of the most iconic and recognisable areas of London, Hong Kong and Shanghai'.

Their website described the brief as 'to take an established, tired garden from the early 20th century into the 21st century while still keeping the old skeleton (including many valuable mature trees) incorporating a simple, classic layout.

The face of The (New) Old Garden looking onto the garden and towards the river, as designed by Quinlan Terry, architect. (Photo by James Brittain)

'The overall framework of the garden was kept with a central axis leading from the house half-way down the garden to a centrally placed "D" which marks the change to differing sections.

'Originally laid out during the mid 1920s, the garden preserves much of its formal layout; original planting has matured to create the most wonderful specimen trees and with considerable investment and further design the gardens are now magnificent. A long central axis leading from the house is flanked by expansive lawns planted with specimen trees, reminiscent of the gardens' former use as part of the pleasure gardens attached to Buccleuch House on the opposite side of the Thames. Halfway down, breedon [soft gravel] and lawn paths flow out in a classic Patte d'Oie (goosefoot), forming an axis to both the swimming pool and yew walk. An elegant, flowing planting scheme leads through the many rooms of the garden: a large pond is a haven for wildlife, informal ecological areas have been developed including a large wildflower meadow, living walls and bat habitats. Herbs and vegetables … can be grown in the ornamental working potager and picking garden. A magnificent 60 metre … herbaceous border draws the eye down through the garden towards the podium and peek-a-boo gate off the towpath, while elements of the earlier garden – the rolling yew hedge walk, and ancient wisterias – have been preserved and renovated so that they now harmoniously combine within the simple classic layout. The ancient wisteria trees, now firmly supported by bespoke solid green oak pergolas, simply take your breath away when in full bloom. Perimeter woodland planting and deep screen planting, in addition to a new garden wall, railings and fencing, have been introduced along the property boundaries to give privacy from the surrounding areas.

'... Nestling within the gardens is the new outdoor swimming pool, surrounded by York stone paving in keeping with the cream stone of the house façade. A championship-sized tennis court has been incorporated into the body of the garden in an open natural lawn setting; its surrounding curtain net can be drawn back to ensure permeability between the wisteria, pool and tennis court spaces.'

The (New) Old Garden, designed by Quinlan Terry, architect. (Photo by James Brittain)

The property particulars continued, stressing the quality of the build and its fittings: 'The impressive residence is arranged over basement, ground, first and second floors with a gross area of approximately 20,000 sq ft. The quality of the building is immediately apparent. Hand crafted and traditionally constructed from French Anstrude limestone, with bespoke hardwood windows and a traditional Welsh slate roof, all materials, reference and detail have been carefully considered to reflect the prestige of the residence. The front courtyard, with ample parking for up to twenty vehicles, is laid with sawn Porphyry granite setts together with York stone paviors that continue through to the east facing garden terrace. Created as a family home, the house has been designed to function simply and efficiently on a day-to-day basis, while incorporating key features such as the grand enfilades and other formal architectural arrangements typical of large country houses.

'Finishes befitting such an elegant house include Portland stone and oak floors, granites and marbles, all installed to the highest standards of workmanship demanded from carefully selected craftsmen. A stunning Portland stone cantilevered staircase runs up through the house, but a lift, should you need one, is also provided. The first floor provides a master suite in excess of 1,200 sq ft with five further family and guest bedrooms all with ensuite facilities. The second floor provides three additional family and guest bedrooms with ensuite facilities together with a large seating area. Staff quarters are accommodated within an independent section of the house on ground and basement levels and are totally self-sufficient. The house is controlled by a sophisticated, combined Crestron and Lutron system and the audio visual, security, IT and phone installations are state-of-the-art and in every room. Underfloor heating provides warmth while the fibrous ceilings, moulded to a Quinlan & Francis Terry classic design, conceal efficient air-cooling throughout the house.

'While The Old Garden boasts an elegant dining room and open-plan drawing room among its principle reception rooms, the latter with French doors out to an expansive entertaining terrace overlooking the gardens, the dominant feature of the house is undoubtedly the magnificent entrance hall. Similar to the Cube Room at the Queen's House, Greenwich (1614–1617), by Inigo Jones, it is a perfect square. The double-height space and arrangement of high windows, doors and decorative stone were influenced by The Great Hall [the entrance to Ditchley Park] in Oxfordshire by Gibbs and Kent (1722) and the decoration on the ceiling of the hall is based on the carving on the Ara Pacis, Rome (9BC). With the perfectly proportioned double-height ceiling, fibrous plaster detailing and striking hand turned timber balustraded gallery, it creates an awe-inspiring first impression.

'Large enough to accommodate a team of chefs should the occasion demand, the kitchen is equally suited for more intimate, family use …

'At the south side of the house, a spectacular 12.5m indoor pool hall opens onto a south-facing sun terrace, with views over the garden and down to the Thames. Additional facilities include a Klaf steam room, a gymnasium and a treatment room, while the garden offers further options for relaxing and leisure pursuits. Besides the staff rooms, laundry room, plant and store rooms located on the lower ground floor, there is a fully racked wine cellar, a tournament-quality snooker room and a state-of-the-art media entertainment room.'

The *Richmond & Twickenham Times* on 12 June 1981 had revealed that the previous Old Garden house was 'on the market for a spectacular £600,000'.

The Telegraph website on 19 September 2012 reported that the new Old Garden was 'sold late last year for £43m to another Russian buyer. According to Tim Hubbard, of buying agent Property Vision, it is now on the market again for £50 million.'

This grand house, with its ultramodern technology, represents the twenty-first century equivalent of the opulent riverside mansions of earlier centuries, such as the Jacobean Cambridge House of four hundred years earlier. The tall oak front gates, and the heavily screened entry point into the garden from the public riverside path, successfully protect the privacy of the owner, hiding it from modern eyes.

Other recent developments in these first two decades of the new century have been far more visible to residents and passers-by, and some of them contentious.

CHAPTER 25
INTO THE 21ST CENTURY AND THE PANDEMIC

Unsurprisingly for a London borough, planning and development issues have continued to stir emotions since the turn of the millennium. The care home at Hatfield House, 40 Cambridge Park, which had previously functioned as a kindergarten, and in the 1930s even as a prep school, was given permission in 2005 to be converted into self-contained apartments, while a new care home was built at the rear to house its existing residents, significantly reducing the size of the gardens. Protests came from neighbours throughout the planning process.

Next door, the owners of No. 40A Cambridge Park submitted plans a few years later to demolish the existing house – possibly a nineteenth-century lodge from the old Cambridge Park mansion itself – and to replace it with six dwellings, three in the basement, and three above, up to two storeys above ground level. Resistance from local residents and some councillors resulted in the plans evolving into a single new-build residence in contemporary style, for which permission was finally granted in 2013.

Hatfield House, 40 Cambridge Park, in 2020, now divided into apartments (Photo by Jonathan Crofts)

Away from planning issues, and less controversially, the London 2012 Olympics saw Richmond Road closed to traffic, and side roads cordoned off with no vehicular access or departure, over the weekend of the trans-city cycling races. The course started and ended in The Mall in central London and took in a loop via Surrey, while the time trials began and finished at Hampton Court Palace. Eighteen events were contested with around five hundred athletes. Residents gathered behind the pink-banner-clad barriers as first police outriders came over the bridge at speed and wove their way along the road, followed by a host of cyclists and support vehicles. After much waiting, they all went past in a flash and East Twickenham's moment of glory was over.

Marshals monitor Richmond Road and the crowds ahead of the arrival of the 2012 Olympic teams, who then descend the slope from Richmond Bridge (Photos by Jonathan Crofts)

MALKIAT SINGH
UBBI

1961-2015

OUR COMMUNITY PHARMACIST
FOR 30 YEARS

(Photos by Jonathan Crofts)

Of more enduring character, Charles Harry was the first chemist (pharmacist) on the corner site at 366 Richmond Road. The original name and façade are preserved to this day, despite a succession of chemists who have since advised the local population from these premises, including through two global pandemics.

'Ubbi' was the resident pharmacist for some three decades, having started work there as a teenager. He died suddenly in 2015 and over one thousand people attended his funeral. Tributes to him poured in from customers and friends:

> *'A huge loss that has left us all speechless and very reflective on the positive impact Ubbi had on our lives, he bought peace in an often disruptive world. RIP'*

Otherwise, Richmond Road businesses are now an eclectic mix, including multiple charity shops, convenience stores, hardware stores, a bicycle shop, laundries, hairdressers and barbers, a nail bar and a school uniform supplier, several dental clinics, an opticians and a pharmacy, estate agents, technology and IT support businesses, a branch of car repair outfit Kwikfit and an MOT repair centre – the last vestiges of vehicle maintenance enterprises along this stretch. All of these nestle alongside the inevitable delis, cafés, fast food outlets and restaurants, even a shisha lounge. While many local residents continue to shop over the bridge in central Richmond, East Twickenham still offers a broad range of services to the local population and for people passing through.

Next to the bus stop heading into Richmond once stood the old housing, retail and office site built by the Thomas Saunders Partnership in 1979 at No. 397 Richmond Road: the 'new' Ryde House and nearby flats. This lay empty from 2006 (other than occasional use as a filming location) and between 2019 and 2021

was redeveloped as a Lidl supermarket and a 'free' school, Deer Park School, after intense scrutiny of the plans from local residents and traders, bringing new flavour to the busy thoroughfare.

Early in the construction process on the Lidl site, concrete was at one point pumped in error into the local sewerage system, instead of the foundations. Drilling out of the pipes proved lengthy and expensive, with waste tankers parked up on Richmond Road for some weeks to dispose of the sewerage, which would otherwise have had nowhere to go – a cause for both consternation and amusement in local streets. Some months later, building slowed again with the advent of an unforeseen and unavoidable source of delay.

A century on from the Spanish flu that had played such havoc with the fortunes of the old Gaiety Cinema, the local community was once again caught in the grip of a global pestilence. In 2020, citizens worldwide found their lives turned upside down by the Covid-19 coronavirus. In the streets covered by the Richmond Bridge Residents' Association, an informal music group sprang up, which coordinated street

Top: The construction of the new Lidl supermarket and school in Richmond Road in 2019-2021. The huge HTC crane became a feature of the landscape in East Twickenham until it was finally dismantled in October 2020, blocking part of Richmond Road for a day.

Bottom: The new Deer Park School drawing closer to completion in 2021. (Old) Ryde House is on the right. (Photos by Jonathan Crofts)

singing just after the nationwide 'Clap for Carers', every Thursday evening at 8pm during the peak of the first wave of infection. Along with the rest of the nation, local residents appeared in front of their houses each week to recognise the intense commitment and personal sacrifice of NHS, care and key workers. Many called for salary raises for 'key workers', rather than symbolic applause.

Over the course of the pandemic, the UK population adopted a new jargon: the 'lockdown', introduced by the government to reduce the risk of infection over successive waves, resulted in traffic becoming sporadic, with walkers and cyclists able to use the full width of the roads as they sought to avoid other people with the recommended 'social distancing'. Citizens queued outside supermarkets, and initially, stocks of lavatory paper, hand sanitiser, baking supplies and paracetamol were in short supply. Many individuals volunteered to help deliver shopping or medicines to elderly or vulnerable people, as those with longterm conditions were asked to 'shield' for many months, barely able to leave their home. Face coverings or masks became commonplace, and were eventually required on public transport and in shops.

Foodbanks found themselves inundated as many families struggled on reduced income with breadwinners 'furloughed', or made redundant as businesses struggled, unable to trade, according to whatever 'tier' of restrictions had been imposed in response to the latest infection 'R rate'. For office-based professionals, the notion of 'homeworking' suddenly became the norm, along with meetings in pyjama bottoms and smart shirts via Zoom video-conferencing. Even children were 'home-schooled' by their parents for long months, with public exams cancelled and results estimated, not to everyone's satisfaction.

Everyone watched in alarm the bulletins delivered by the prime minister, Boris Johnson, and his advisers, with updates on infection rates and mounting deaths. The whole nation suddenly understood the meaning of the term 'exponential rise'. Scandals came and went, as yet again, some of those in power found themselves outside the rules for everyone else.

Military Chinook helicopters could be heard overhead and the occasional army lorry was spotted on the streets, delivering essential supplies of PPE (personal protective equipment) or vaccines to health and social care settings. Mass testing centres were set up behind Twickenham Stadium and in the Old Deer Park at Richmond.

The airspace above, normally dominated by the roar of jets heading into and out of Heathrow Airport, fell eerily quiet for a while, with flights heavily restricted. Contrails across the vivid blue sky were cause for remark, and birdsong and the chirrup of insects in the glorious spring to autumn of 2020 all at once seemed deafening. Gardens and parks blossomed in extraordinary abundance – the effect of one of nature's mast (bumper crop) years.

Widening of Richmond Road pavements to promote social distancing during the Covid-19 pandemic in 2020–2021 (Photo by Jonathan Crofts)

In East Twickenham, the pavements along Richmond Road were extended by temporary bollards to allow more space for pedestrians alongside pinch points such as the bus stop. Cycle lanes were fortified to encourage as many people as possible to take to two wheels, and avoid public transport. Richmond Bridge itself became one-way on the pavements, or in theory at least. Somehow life continued, albeit largely behind closed doors.

Away from the stresses of life and closer to the timeless river, however, part of the original lawns of Cambridge House offer solace in the form of Cambridge Gardens – a popular local park and playground overlooking Richmond Bridge and neighbouring the site of the former Richmond Ice Rink and Richmond Bridge Works. Instead of the derelict public lavatories, there is now a café serving tennis courts with coaching facilities, and space for the public of all generations. The surrounding community set up the Friends of Cambridge Gardens, 'to help enhance this green and make it a beautiful breathing space'. The group also oversees the well-being of Warren Gardens, and at the time of writing is seeking funding jointly with RiBRA (Richmond Bridge Residents' Association) for the renovation of the strip of ground at the end of Denton Road with wildlife-friendly planting and a stag-beetle loggery.

The whole stretch of gardens, residential and municipal, also form part of the linear corridor along the river, allowing bats and other wildlife to travel between different open zones through the centre of London. As the Thames Landscape Strategy notes: 'The River Thames is one of the most important habitats for bats in southern England acting as a huge larder for these nocturnal mammals that feast on the midges and mosquitoes buzzing over the water: a single bat can eat a staggering two thousand in one night. The bats roost in the old veteran trees in nearby parks, navigating their way to the river via the "bat super-highways" that link the river with the open spaces. The Thames is home to seven species of bats including noctule, Daubenton's and pipistrelle, although their numbers are constantly at threat from development, bad lighting and habitat loss.'

There have been numerous and ongoing changes over the last century, but it is still possible in our own time to appreciate the vision and enterprise of the two Victorian speculative builders, Jeremiah Little and Henry Foulkes, who between them were responsible for the creation, in their individual styles, of such a large part of the suburb of East Twickenham.

Large-scale construction projects, such as the supermarket and school, will doubtless continue to alter the local landscape. The economic effects of the Covid-19 pandemic, together with the impact of the new supermarket, will affect the composition of local shops and businesses along the Richmond Road. The primary school will nurture many of the younger children of the surrounding area and beyond.

Green initiatives may well change the function or appearance of the roads and traffic, and a proposed relaxation of building planning regulations may have an impact, but the leafiness and friendly feel of many of the neighbourhood roads and of Cambridge and Warren Gardens and the river towpath, are likely to remain protected. Local organisations such as Richmond Bridge Residents' Association (RiBRA) and the Friends of Cambridge Gardens will continue to press for active involvement in planning debates.

However the Cambridge Park neighbourhood evolves in the future, more stories of the lives, businesses and buildings of influential residents and traders will emerge, and its people will continue to cherish their home.

The history and character of these few special streets make it too valued a part of London and the Arcadian Thames for anything less.

Richmond Road and the
corner of Morley Road,
early 1900s
(Postcard image provided
by Alan Winter)

(Richmond upon Thames
Local Studies Library
and Archive)

AFTERWORD

'Although the reader may have found in the preceding pages little to engage his attention by the recital of great events, to provoke emulation by the display of profound erudition or to excite industry by the example of intense study, I still presume to hope that these memoirs may have their use, by furnishing that class of men to which my father belonged, men of easy and independent fortunes who have a taste for the liberal arts, and a relish for the pleasures of polished life, with a practical example of one who succeeded to the utmost of his wishes in the attainment of rational happiness; from whose experience they may learn that the enjoyments of the world are not inconsistent either with religion or virtue, with philosophical retirement, or with domestic happiness; and that the favour of the great, the esteem of the learned, and the admiration of the witty, may be obtained without any undue concessions, or any departure from those principles, which should govern a wise man and a good Christian.'

Archdeacon George Owen Cambridge, writing of his father Richard Owen Cambridge
Twickenham Meadows, 1 June 1803

APPENDICES

APPENDIX A

Land inherited by Joseph Windham Ashe (via his wife Martha Ashe) in 1734, and subsequently mortgaged to Valens Comyns on 21 April 1742. (GLRO ACC 1379/41)

1. All that customary messuage with Barns Stables Pigeon House Buildings Orchards Gardens etc. in Twickenham near Richmond Ferry

2. 50 acres of copyhold land in Warren Close alternately Old Warren adjoining the messuage

3. 12 acres in Long and Short Sandborough Closes (3 acres formerly lands of Thomas Lawley; 3 ½ acres formerly William Ossifers; 2 'half-acres' formerly Richard Ells; half acre formerly Ralph Blowers; 1 acre formerly Edward Birkheads; 2 acres Robert Bartletts)

4. Ten Acre Close (formerly Robert Bartletts then Thomas Lawleys)

5. 3 ½ acres lying in Coney Furlong (half acre formerly Robert Bartletts; half acre formerly William Ossifers; 2 acres ex Richard Ells; half acre Thomas Lawleys.)

6. 7 ⅓ acres of copyhold land in Short Farthingworth Close acres formerly John Bartletts; ½ acre Charles Pitcarne; ½ acre ex William Whites; half acre ex Edmund Prescotts; ⅔ acre ex George Bartletts; ⅔ acre ex Thomas ??)

7. Five acres in Westbay Close (alt. Highway Shott) 1 acre ex Henry Poultons; 1 acre ex Thomas Smiths; 1 acre ex Thomas Gees; 2 acres Richard Ells.)

8. Six acres in Bakers Orchard Close.

9. Three acres in Longfarthingworth Shot, late David Battys.

10. 1 acre purchased of Thomas Gee

11. 2 ½ acres in Guy's Hedge Close formerly Thomas Cole

12. Half acre purchased of Charles Pitcarne

13. ⅔ acre purchased of Thomas Cole

14. Half acre purchased of William White

15. Half acre purchased of Executors of Henry Poulton

16. ⅔ purchased of George Bartlett

17. One acre purchased of Edward Bartlett

18. And also 1 acre of ... Smith

APPENDIX B

Disposal of Ashe Lands after 1747 by Valens Comyn and later Richard Comyn.

9 Oct. 1747 Six acres in Bakers Orchard (alt. Longfarthingworth Nursery) to George Morton Pitt, of Orleans House.

[now the site of Orleans School]

13 Apr. 1748 7 ⅓ acres in Short Farthingworth Close, to The Countess of Suffolk.

(the corner of Richmond Road and Montpelier Row)

13 Jan. 1752 Messuage nr. Richmond Ferry (with pigeon-house, buildings etc)

50 acres in Warren Close or Old Warren

12 acres in Long and Short Sandborough Closes

Close nr. messuage called Ten Acre Close to Charles Yorke and Robert Kingscote as Trustees of the Family Settlement for Richard Owen Cambridge [Cambridge Park]

17 Apr. 1754 3 ½ acres in close called Coney Furlong. [This land lay between the Rising Sun and Sandycoombe Road.]

5 acres in Westbay Close

3 acres in Long Farthingworth Shot

2 ½ acres in Guy's Hedge Close (alt. Little Dottin Piece)

1 acre purchased of Thomas Gee

Half acre purchased of Charles Pitcarne

⅔ acre purchased of Thomas Cole

Half acre of William White

Half acre of Ralph Blower

Half acre purchased of Executors of Henry Poulton

Half acre purchased of John Bartlett

⅔ acre purchased of George Bartlett

1 acre purchased of Edward Bartlett to Joshua Spyers.

APPENDIX C

Tablet of the Ashe family

'In a vault underneath this monument lieth the body of Sir Joseph Ashe of Twittenham Bart IVth son of James Ashe of the County of Sommerset Esquire descended from the antient family of the Ashes of Devonshire

He married Mary daughter of Mr. Robt Wilson of Low Mercht. He had by her 2 sons, Joseph and James and vii daughters, Catherinne married to William Windham of Norfolk Esqure, Mary the late wife of Horatio Lord Viscount Townshend, Anne, Martha, Grace, Elizabeth and Diana. He died the XV April MDCLXXXVI in the LXIX year of his age, his wife and IV children, James, Catherinne, Anne, Martha, surviving him. Mary Ashe relict of Sir Joseph Ashe Bart departed this life 28th November 1705 in the 74th year of her age and lyeth interred in this vault.

In this vault lyeth the body of Martha Ashe 4th daughter of Sir Joseph Ashe who departed this life ye 1st August 1714 in ye 57th year of her Age.'

Tablet of the Cambridge Family

'In the adjoining ground are deposited the earthly remains of Richard Owen Cambridge Esqr who died September 17th, 1802; aged 86 years, with Mary his wife, daughter of George Trenchard Esqr of Woolveton, Dorset, who survived her husband, after a happy union of 61 years, in the 90th year of her age, Septr. the 11th 1806. And two maiden daughters, Charlotte, born June 10th, 1746, died March 25th, 1823, Catherine, born November 19th, 1750, died June 7th, 1784, with Richard Owen Cambridge, grandson of the above, who died October 6th, 1775; aged 9 years. In the same vault are deposited the remains of the Rev. George Owen Cambridge, M.A., Archdeacon of Middlesex and Prebendary of Ely, who died May 1st, 1841. Aged 85'

St Mary's Church, Twickenham, also known as St Mary the Virgin, Church Street, Twickenham, where the Ashe and Cambridge families' tablets are located, January 2021 (Photo by Jonathan Crofts)

ACKNOWLEDGEMENTS & SOURCES

I am deeply indebted to Maureen Bunch whose two Borough of Twickenham Local History Society (BOTLHS) papers (No. 63, *Cambridge Park, Twickenham, and its Owners 1616–1835*, and No. 68, *Cambridge Park, East Twickenham, The Building of a Suburb*) form the basis of the early period covered in this book. Maureen was writing some thirty years ago, and is sadly no longer with us. I would dearly have liked to have met her.

Also to Mike Cherry and the Publications Committee of BOTLHS for giving me permission to adapt her content, and for advice and support with my own research. My sources also include *When The Bombs Fell* by Paul Barnfield (BOTLHS paper 80), and content from the Twickenham Museum website with which BOTLHS is closely connected.

I am of course enormously grateful to Sir Vince Cable for his perceptive Foreword, and to Twickenham artist Simon Broom for the use of his portrait of Sir Vince.

To Bill Rogers, author at Caton Books Ltd, for financial sponsorship towards production costs.

And to my editor, Monica Byles, and designer, Annie Rushton, for their support, insight and experience, and generously given time.

My sincere thanks also goes to (in no particular order):

Dr Helen Baker, Chair and Research Lead of the East Twickenham Centennial Group, who provided a substantial part of the content for the chapter on the Belgian Village, and additional information on the Ice Rink. Helen is also chair of the Friends of Cambridge Gardens;

The REIC (Richmond Environmental Information Centre) and Trustees Teresa Read, Berkley Driscoll and Jeremy Hamilton-Miller for the use of their research and information, including local photographs from the REIC Heritage Lottery Fund project 'The Most Famous Ice Rink in the World', in the chapter on the Richmond Ice Rink;

Various members of the *East Twickenham & St Margarets History* and *Twickenham & Teddington History* Facebook groups, and the *Memories of Richmond Ice Rink* Facebook group, who shared stories and facts from their own personal experiences;

Tony Beckles Willson and the Twickenham Museum for the chapter on the Glass House, and the Museum's sources for other research (www.twickenham-museum.org.uk);

Colin Hines, Dave Wilson and the Twickenham Park Residents Association for the chapter on the Gaiety Cinema and Billiard Hall (www.twickenhampark.co.uk);

David King, local historian, for information and images on the Richmond Ice Rink;

Charles Lawrence, Archivist of the Fairey Owners Club and Ken Merron, son of Arthur Merron, for their support with the history of Merron Ltd. at the Richmond Bridge Works;

Martyn Day and Peter Mahnke of the St Margarets Community Website (www.stmargarets.london) for the Second World War bombing and 1928 flooding excerpts and other information;

Annie Notman and David Parish at St Stephen's Church (www.st-stephens.org.uk) for additional history and photos in the chapter on the church;

RiBRA (Richmond Bridge Residents' Association, www.richmondbridgeresidentsassociation.com) for their support and encouragement;

Rachel Morrison and the team at English Heritage (and to the British Library website, www.bl.uk) for the chapter on Artists and Perspectives, and other shared research via *Marble Hill Remembers* (November 2020 Remembrance exhibition) and its exemplary team of volunteers;

London Transport Museum and the Museum of London Archaeology Service for additional history on the bus garage;

British Pathé newsreels for their content on the Richmond Bridge Works fire of 1948;

Janine Stanford, Archivist at Richmond Local Studies, for information on the Richmond Bridge Works and Beaufort Works companies, and her extensive help with illustrations;

Andrew Tweedie, Editor, and *Grace's Guide to British Industrial History* (www.gracesguide.co.uk) for information on the engineering and commercial works sites;

Thames Landscape Strategy (thames-landscape-strategy.org.uk) for information on the Thames corridor;

Keith Whitworth and Keith Whitworth Architects for information and images about Meadowbank;

Quinlan Terry and Quinlan Terry Architects for the chapter and images about The (New) Old Garden;

Jeannie Benjamin and *War Widows Stories* (warwidowsstories.org.uk) for the post-war memories of Haversham Grange;

Dr George Simmers and his Great War Fiction blog (greatwarfiction.wordpress.com) for information and images about Ernie Lotinga;

The Mary Groombridge estate for artefacts and stories from her life;

John Watson for information on the Beaufort Works;

For help with illustrations: Chris Burton at the Richmond Borough Art Collection/ Orleans House Gallery; Christie's Images Limited; Collection of the Duke of Northumberland; Delphis Antiques; Historic England; *Illustrated London News*/Mary Evans Picture Library; Kenneth Lea; London Transport Museum; National Library of Scotland; National Portrait Gallery (London); National Trust; *Richmond & Twickenham Times*; Royal Museum of the Armed Forces and Military History, Belgium; Scottish National Portrait Gallery; Sotheby's; Howard Webb; Alan Winter; Roger Wyer; and many other local individuals;

And anyone else from the local community, all of whom have been more than generous with their time and information.

Other sources include:

Aldwych Speed Club website (www.aldwychspeedclub.com)

Ancestry (ancestry.co.uk)

Arcadian Thames, Mavis Batey, Henrietta Buttery, David Lambert, Kim Wilkie (Barn Elms, 1994)

The British Library website (www.bl.uk)

The Coloured Mass, David G C Allan (BOTLHS, 2011)

Crossing the River: the History of London's Thames River Bridges from Richmond to the Tower, Brian Cookson, (Transworld, 2015)

Electronics & Wireless World magazine, August 1985

The Government Art Collection website (www.artcollection.culture.gov.uk)

History of Parliament website (www.historyofparliamentonline.org)

IMDb, the Internet Movie Database (www.imdb.com)

J.M.W. Turner and the 'Matchless Vale of Thames', Catherine Parry-Wingfield (Turner's House Trust, 2020)

London United Tramways: A History 1894–1933, Geoffrey Wilson (Routledge, 1971)

The Making of Modern Twickenham, J M Lee (Historical Publications, 2005)

The Most Famous Ice Rink In The World, Teresa Read, Berkley Driscoll and David Lane (Legends Publishing, 2015)

Oxford National Dictionary of Biography website (www.oxforddnb.com)

'The Pelabon Munitions works and the Belgian village on the Thames: community and forgetfulness in outer-metropolitan suburbs', *Immigrants & Minorities*, Volume 34, Issue: 2, 151–170, Christophe Declercq & Helen Baker (2016)

Property particulars for The Old Garden, 2014

A Prospect of Richmond, Janet Dunbar (Michael Joseph, 1979)

Randle Siddeley website (www.randlesiddeley.co.uk)

Twickenham Past, Donald Simpson (Historical Publications, 1993)

Twicknam Parke, A C B Urwin (1965)

UK Parliament website (www.edm.parliament.uk)

Une Cité Belge sur la Tamise, Justin Wallon (Librairie Moderne, 1917)

The Works of Richard Owen Cambridge Esq., George Owen Cambridge (1803)

YouTube (www.youtube.com) 'Farewell Richmond Ice Rink 1992', video, posted 9 January 2018 by Mick Angel

Maureen Bunch's two original BOTLHS papers include sources from:

Altick, R D   *R.O. Cambridge; Belated Augustan*, 1941

Bell, Q (Ed.)   *Virginia Woolf, Vol. I*, 1881–1912

Biographical Dictionary of British Architects 1600–1840

Borough of Twickenham Local History Society (BOTLHS)
        Papers: Nos. 8, 31, 35, 41, 58 and 60
        No. 4 (Occasional Paper) 'York House, Twickenham'
        No. 21 'Mrs. Alford Remembers'
        No. 53 'Richard Cobbett's Twickenham 1866–1872'
        No. 63 'Cambridge Park & Its Owners 1616–1835'
        No. 95 'Bloomsbury in Twickenham'

Bygone Twickenham, BOTLHS 1983

Burke's Extinct & Dormant Baronetcies, 1838

Cable & Wireless Co. archives

Cambridge, G O   *R.O. Cambridge; An Account of His Life and Character*, 1803

Cambridge Park House Auction catalogue, 23 October 1902

Census for England & Wales 1871 and 1881

Chancellor, E B   *History & Antiquities of Richmond*, 1894

Cobbett, R S   *Memorials of Twickenham*, 1872

Cockayne, G E   *The Complete Peerage*, 1887

Cooke, W B   *Handbook for Richmond & Twickenham*, 1842

Courage Breweries archives

Dictionary of National Biography

European Magazine 1803, vol. LXIV

Evans, Dr J   *Richmond and Its Vicinity*, 1825

The Gardener's Magazine, 1837, Vol. 13

Gascoigne, B   *Images of Twickenham*, 1981

Gentleman's Magazine, LXXXIII

Greater London Records Office (GLRO)

Hearth Tax Assessment (Twickenham Library)

Henry Little's obituary   *The Middlesex* Chronicle, 18 April 1914

Hodgson, F C   *Thames-side in the Past*, 1913

Ideal Home magazine, June 1926

Illustrated London News, 1869

An Inventory of the Historical Monuments of Middlesex, 1937

Ironside, E   *History & Antiquities of Twickenham*, 1797

Keane, W   *Beauties of Middlesex*, 1849/50

Ketton-Cremer, W *Felbrigg, the Story of a House*, Futura edition, 1982

Kelly's Street Directories, 1897–1928

Kilpatrick, S   *Fanny Burney*, 1980

Lysons, Revd D   *Environs of London*, 1800

Meadow Bank Auction catalogue, June 1877

Pine, L G   *New Extinct Peerage*, 1872

Public Records Office, Chancery Lane (PRO)

Richmond Reference Library

Richmond & Twickenham Times

Royal Institute of British Architects Library

Ryskamp, C and Pottle, F A (eds.)   *Boswell, The Ominous Years: 1774–1776*, 1963

St Stephen's Church

A Short History (and Catalogue) of the Richmond Bridge Bicentenary Exhibition, LBRUT

A Short View of the Principal Seats and Gardens in and about Twickenham, by Mrs. Henrietta Pye, 1755

Somerset House (Family Records Centre)

St Mary's Church, Twickenham, parish church registers, records and vestry minutes

Survey of London, vol. XXXVII (N. Kensington) 1973

Thames Valley Times

The Times, 23 July 1908

Title Deeds 'The Old Garden'

Trease, G   *Portrait of a Cavalier*, 1979

Twickenham Enclosure Award, 1818 (Twickenham Library)

Twickenham Library, Local Studies Room

Twickenham poor rate books (Twickenham Library)

Twickenham UDC Council Minutes and Clerk's Memoranda

Urwin, A C B   *Twicknam Parke*, 1965

Victoria County Histories of Middlesex, Warwickshire and Wiltshire

Wallon, J   *Une Cité Belge sur la Tamise*

Walpole, H   *Correspondence*, edited by Prof. W S Lewis, Oxford University Press

Wentworth Papers 1833, p. 333

Will of Cornelia Cambridge dated 18 March 1851 (Somerset House)

Wilson, G   *London United Tramways*, 1971

Wiltshire Records Office 490/909

Windham family tree (supplied by D Simpson)

INDEX

Right: Richmond Bridge seen from East Twickenham riverside (Warren Footpath), then and now (Above: Howard Webb Collection. Below: Photo by Jonathan Crofts)

Richmond Bridge.

THE AUTHOR

Jonathan Crofts has lived in the Cambridge Park area of East Twickenham since 1993, and has followed local history ever since through reading, talks, walks and visits, as well as his own research and photography. He has amassed an extensive collection of local antique prints.

After leaving Bristol University with a degree in Modern Languages, he embarked on a career in theatre and television, including sixteen years at the BBC, and latterly working all over the world as a consultant with media and broadcast organisations.

During ten years in drama production for the BBC, he once used the office building facing the end of his road as a location to represent the interior of a police station. In 2021, this site became the new Lidl supermarket and Deer Park School on Richmond Road.

His wife Monica Byles has spent over thirty years in book publishing, both fiction and non-fiction, and has guided and supported Jonathan in the production of this book, including the final edit.

Her uncle and grandfather, in the twentieth century, made use of East Twickenham riverside's The Exiles Club (originally and latterly Meadowbank), as engineers employed by its then owner, Cable and Wireless Ltd.

The day Jonathan and Monica moved into their house, they were welcomed on the doorstep by a bouquet of flowers from neighbours two houses away who had lived in the road since the 1960s. That kind gesture set the tone for their tenure of nearly thirty years in the neighbourhood.

One of their neighbours, designer Annie Rushton, later became a friend and has designed this book.

Meadows, Mansions and Munitions is a tribute to the people of Cambridge Park, East Twickenham, as much as a reflection of its history, buildings and gardens.